THE COMMUNITY BUILDING COMPANION

50 Ways to Make Connections & Create Change in Your Own Backyard

Peter D. Rogers, PhD • Lisa Frankfort, LMFT • Matthew McKay, PhD

NEW HARBINGER PUBLICATIONS, INC.

Publisher's Note

Distributed in the U.S.A. by Publishers Group West; in Canada by Raincoast Books; in Great Britain by Airlift Book Company, Ltd.; in South Africa by Real Books, Ltd.; in Australia by Boobook; and in New Zealand by Tan dem Press.

Copyright © 2002 by Peter Rogers, Lisa Frankfort, and Matthew McKay
New Harbinger Publications, Inc.
5674 Shattuck Avenue
Oakland, CA 94609

Cover design by Amy Shoup
Cover image by G & M David de Lossey/The Image Bank
Edited by Clancy Drake
Text design by Michele Waters

ISBN 1-57224-288-4 Paperback

New Harbinger Publications' Web site address: www.newharbinger.com

04   03   02

10   9   8   7   6   5   4   3   2   1

First printing

For the community of those who showed uncommon decency to Jews during World War II, and particularly for Angela Pohl Manthe, who saved the life of Denny Rosenbaum.

—P. D. R.

For Patrick Horay, who has given so much to so many.

—M. M.

My deepest thanks to: my mother for being my role model; my father for his pride in me; Joan and Donna for their stories; Matt and Peter for this opportunity; Gus for always being in my corner; and Teddy, who always played well with others.

—L. F.

CONTENTS

Nearly thirty years ago, I met a man named Walter Lipton. He was a social worker whose caseload was exclusively made up of chronic schizophrenics. Walter's clients never really got better, but he worked tirelessly to improve the quality of their daily lives.

The thing that stood out about Walter, above all, was his cheerfulness. And that never changed, even when he was diagnosed with ALS, even when he spoke with a slur and could no longer move his arms. "What is it," I once asked him, "that makes you happier than most people I know—despite this disease?"

I knew the answer before I heard him say it. I knew because he'd already shown me that the secret ingredient to a happy life is to "get involved." Walter was part of at least a dozen organizations devoted to improving society in one way or another, and he used to drag me off to the meetings so I could "get involved," too. Whether it was a neighborhood enhancement committee, a food co-op, the Railway Passenger Association, or a group promoting social justice, Walter was a full participant. And his involvement with others helped him stay positive and focused, no matter how physically weak he became.

Walter was, and remains, a model for me. But more than that, he inspired this book, because his brand of community building is what many of the stories you'll read here are all about.

Community building can take many forms. Walter's kind of group, focused on improving society, is just one of them. Many of the groups you'll learn about here provide support to overcome personal problems—either physical or emotional. Others focus on a common activity that brings people together, with no higher ambition than giving folks an opportunity for sharing and enjoyment.

Take your choice. But whatever you do, throw yourself into it. Get involved. Let the stories here inspire you, give you ideas. Let them show you the way to make communities of your own.

—Matthew McKay
Nance's Hot Springs
Calistoga, California

THE STORIES

FOOD BUYING GROUP

It was the eggs. That's how it all got started. Sally had grown up on a farm in the Midwest. She really missed the taste of fresh eggs. And she was tired of the poor choices available at her local store. Sally knew that all retail food stores, not just the big chains, conspire to provide us with the lowest quality food at the highest possible price. They "rotate" their stock so that we're always buying the least fresh food available (i.e., the food that's closest to its expiration date).

Sally knew there were farmer's markets, and decided to check one out for herself. There was nothing available locally during the week, but she found out about one that was open early Saturday mornings not more than a twenty-minute drive south of where she lived. When she arrived at the farmer's market, sure enough, there was a stall that featured fresh eggs still warm from the chicken coop. But there was a catch: the eggs were being sold only by the flat. A flat holds thirty eggs, more than even her egg-loving family could consume in a timely fashion.

The solution was obvious. She needed to find other people who liked fresh eggs, and who would take turns making the early morning run to the farmer's market. When her best friend, Maxine, came over for coffee on Monday, Sally broached the topic. As it turned out, Maxine was interested in getting really fresh organic fruits and vegetables, also available at the farmer's market. They both agreed to canvass their neighbors to see if there were others with similar interests.

The following Sunday afternoon found the two friends each walking down one side of their street, going door to door with clipboards in hand. When they met later on to compare notes, they found that, all in all, ten other families were interested in further exploring the idea. The next step was a potluck dessert meeting in Sally's large downstairs rumpus room. At the appointed time, representatives from eight other families showed up. Sally chaired the meeting. She began by saying that the purpose of this neighborhood food buying group was not to replace "regular" shopping, but to provide families with the freshest fruits, vegetables, and eggs possible. She asked the group for a commitment to try out the idea for a month. She and Maxine had figured that the shoppers would need about $100 a week to make the trip to the farmer's market worthwhile. That came down to $10 per week per family, and that amount was readily agreed upon by the group. Maxine agreed to collect the money and keep records of moneys spent.

The next item on the agenda was to set up guidelines for what to buy. Everyone had their own favorites, of course. However, they all agreed that it would be best to buy whatever was in season, and hopefully at a discount. It was also agreed that every effort would be made to honor special requests. Sally observed that with ten members, they could buy exactly four flats of eggs, providing each family with an even dozen.

The last item of business was to make up a rotation schedule for "shoppers of the week," and to set the time and place for families to pick up the food each Saturday. The basic idea was that two members of the group would pair up each week; one of the shoppers in each pair had to have either a pickup truck or a van. They would make the best purchases available at the farmer's market, then return to one of their houses and divide up the haul into ten equal portions. The food would be available on the front lawn (or in the garage in case of rain) by noon that day.

Joe, a bachelor, picked up a supply of empty wooden wine boxes near the Dumpster behind K & L Wine Shoppe to help sort the produce. Sally had saved lots of empty egg cartons, which the group would use to redistribute the flats of eggs. And Maggie had a year's supply of used paper bags. They were all set.

The next Saturday, Sally and Maxine made the first food run. They were up at the crack of dawn, armed with a thermos of coffee and ten crisp ten-dollar bills. A couple of hours later they were contentedly filling the ten wooden boxes with a cornucopia of goodies. "Oohs" and "aahs" filled the air as families came by to pick up their share. And Sally made great tasting huevos rancheros on Sunday.

To create a successful food buying group:

- Get together the right-size group—a minimum of eight families and a maximum of twelve is about right.

- If a large family (more that four people) wants to join, they may wish to buy an additional share, and to double their work commitment. So, in Sally and

Maxine's group, a large family would contribute $20 a week and shop twice as often as other group members.

- For rainy days, a covered vehicle (a truck with a camper shell or a van) must be available, as well as a covered pickup area (like an empty garage or carport).

- Make sure the group shares a common philosophy of what foods are "good," and keep a list of strong likes and dislikes.

THE DIEGO RIVERA COMMUNITY GARDEN

The smell of lavender infuses the air all along the border of the west-side fence of the Diego Rivera Community Garden. Directly under the garden's sign, a row of Rivera's signature calla lilies creates another border. On the east side four varieties of roses—Voodoos, Sunbrights, Cary Grants, and Angel Faces—bow gently in the breeze, turning their opened faces up toward the sun. Rosario Morales hands a basket to her friend Maria Theresa. "Here, take this," she says. "Those tomatoes of yours are ready to drop. That happens? Gets ugly fast." The two women grin at each other. "Tomato sandwiches for lunch," Maria Theresa says invitingly. "Ahhh. Your tomatoes? I can eat one like an apple," Rosario confides with a beatific smile.

"Hi, girls!" calls a voice and both women look down the neatly terraced row of the garden. Tina Gonzales is only fifteen; the women, both fifty years her senior, thoroughly enjoy the affectionate greeting.

"Hey you," calls Rosario, giving the girl a warm smile. A year ago Tina lost her beloved father to cancer, and the garden has been a way for her to process her grief and honor her dad, who loved the outdoors and believed in the healing aspect of nature. Both Rosario and Maria Theresa taught Tina about gardening, everything from how and when to plant potatoes, lettuce, or daisies to mulching and weeding.

Tina wipes a strand of hair off her forehead then pulls on a pair of gardening gloves. "Hey, Maria Theresa. You should probably pick some of those tomatoes soon, huh."

"Thanks for your ex-per-tise. Guess what you're having for lunch, missy!"

"I'm picking raspberries today and my mom's coming by from the corner store with whipped cream. That's my contribution," says Tina, and darts over to the far fence, where her raspberry bushes flourish, their sharp thorns discouraging unwanted visitors. Rosario pulls a carrot out of the ground and brushes the dirt gently from its skin. "I'm always hungry when I come here," she says to Maria Theresa. "Now why is that?" She places the carrot in the basket and moves on to check the progress of some squash.

- Decide what kind of garden you want to have. Will it be a flower garden or one with bushes, vegetables, and fruit trees as well as flowers? Who will be the people involved? Could anyone have a plot there, or does the community want the garden to have a particular purpose, such as teaching gardening to children, or growing organic produce? A community garden can be anything you want it to be, as long as the decisions are thought through up front and the people it will serve are involved in the planning process.

- Gardens are not cheap to maintain, particularly if the garden will serve low-income or retired people. The community garden can charge a maintenance fee or membership dues, but it is helpful—and sometimes essential—to have a sponsor. Money is not the only thing that can be provided by a sponsor: donations of tools, supplies, and even the land for the garden could be provided by your city or county, a private owner, or your local garden and landscaping store or lumberyard.

- Select an appropriate site for the garden (if it has not been provided by your city). Make sure that the plot of land will get enough sunlight for your needs and that it has ready access to water. If you are leasing the land, three years may be a good time span to shoot for.

- Decide how many plots the land can reasonably accommodate, and involve others in readying the site for planting. Delegating is important, since this will not be a full-time job for anyone and there will be much to do in terms of preparing the soil, designing the layout of the garden, marking the plots, and creating a place to store tools and bags of soil.

STILLWELL NEIGHBORS' IMPROVEMENT SOCIETY

In March, 1942, the drifts were up to fifteen feet in the mountains of Grayson County, Virginia. Mrs. Weaver, lying in an isolated cabin, was preparing to give birth to her sixth child. The problem was, she needed a cesarean, and the George Ben Johnson Memorial Hospital was fifty miles away in Abingdon.

A call was made to the nearest station requesting that they hold Train 202, which at that moment was getting ready to depart. In the meantime, neighbors fastened a mattress to a two-horse sled, and began moving Mrs. Weaver along the freezing, five-mile journey to that waiting train. Within a few hundred yards, the horses broke through a sheet of ice and got stuck. So the neighbors—nearly fifty men, women, and kids—pulled and pushed that sled down a perilous mountain track for almost three hours. At the end, they found Train 202 still waiting, and engineer Ben Ball pushed it to the limit in a non-stop run to Abingdon.

The story of Mrs. Weaver (and seven-pound Richard Norwest Weaver) is really what community is all about. It's about people being there for each other. Helping and keeping each other safe. Giving support and comfort, sometimes at great personal cost. These days, it's a rare thing for neighbors to be a real community. We lock our doors and watch a lot of cable. Often we aren't aware of the needs and struggles of people just a few houses away.

Recently, a movement has been growing to bring the spirit of Grayson County circa 1942 into our urban neighborhoods. It goes by a lot of names—community builders, helping hands, good neighbors, fix-it friends—but the core idea is the same. Folks pool their energy, talents, and resources to help neighbors in need. Some community builders focus their efforts on a target population, for example, seniors on fixed incomes whose homes cry out for repair. Others prioritize fixable problems in the homes and apartments of any neighbor who seeks help.

There's a large apartment building in West Oakland, California, that illustrates how community builders can make a difference. It started, as neighborhood organizations often do, with a party. A few tenants organized a Fourth of July ribs and corn cookout in a vacant lot next to their building. There was a good crowd—a lot of laughter. But there was also an undertone of anger. Folks were seething because the building was falling apart and the landlord refused to fix anything. Then and there, the Stillwell Neighbors' Improvement Society was formed. About ten people do most of the work—usually for about three hours on Saturday mornings. They'll do anything: paint, build shelves, fix a lock, get an oven working. Last week they were in the fifth-floor apartment of a single mom. Several neighbors painted the living room, one replaced the glass in a broken window, one screwed new legs on an ancient couch, and one worked on restoring electricity to the nine-year-old's bedroom.

Around noon, the neighbor being helped usually cooks up a little something for his or her hardworking friends. It's a nice tradition, and there's a lot of laughter and good feeling during lunch.

If you'd like to create your own Stillwell Neighbors' Improvement Society, we suggest you:

- Start with a block or apartment party.

- Personally invite each person there to the first meeting. Give special attention and encouragement to people with construction skills.

- Survey your neighbors to find out who needs help.

- Create a priority list, starting with improvements that can be done easily and cheaply: things that'll take no more than one or two mornings to complete. The reason to start small is so you can build on success.

- Start with improvements that are obvious—something the whole neighborhood will notice. Painting a front porch, fixing stairs, or trimming an overgrown garden are examples.

- Send out flyers letting neighbors know the time, location, and nature of the next project and summarizing what was accomplished in the last one.

- Try to set the same time each weekend for your neighborhood projects so folks can build it into their schedules. Save time afterward for eating and socializing—it's the reward for all that hard work.

EDUCATIONAL BLOCK PARTY

It is rare that we can pinpoint exactly when an idea occurred to us. This one is easy, however. The tornado hit a few minutes after noon on June 8th, 1994. Roxanne found herself unprepared, and scared. Meanwhile, on the other side of the street, Sophie, who was new in town, felt alone and unsupported. When the wind and rain finally died down, the two women found themselves looking at each other from their respective soggy front yards.

They got together for coffee the next day and started talking about how to get people prepared for future emergencies on a practical level, and also how to create a caring and supportive group of neighbors. Roxanne agreed to do research on emergency preparedness, and Sophie agreed to research the steps necessary to have a block party. Their idea was to invite all the families on the block for an afternoon of food, and education. Everyone would be encouraged to bring out their lawn chairs and barbecues. There would be face painting for the children, a communal dessert table, and a booth with emergency preparedness information. Sophie and Roxanne agreed to co-chair the event. In order to get a maximum turnout, they decided to stage the block party to coincide with July Fourth.

Sophie went to the local police station and in response to her question about block parties, got a temporary street closure application. Signing the form included meant agreeing to hold the city "harmless" from any and all damages resulting from the temporary street closure. The application included questions concerning the chairperson of the activity, a description of the activity, which street was to be closed (and its nearest intersecting streets), the date and hours of the proposed closure, the estimated number of people, and whether any gifts or gratuities would be solicited.

Sophie also had to indicate whether food, beverages, or merchandise would be on sale and answer questions about sound systems, parking, and traffic barricades. Whew!

Getting the city permit also required the signed approval for the closure of a majority of the residents on the block. This suited Sophie just fine: it gave her an excuse to meet and talk with all of her neighbors on the block. The next morning she began by making a diagram of all the houses on the block. After lunch one day, armed with a clipboard and a sign-up sheet, Sophie began to canvass her neighbors. Anyone she missed, she added to a list of households to contact on the weekend. Within a week Sophie had made personal contact with most of her neighbors, and a majority had approved the street closure.

The block party was a big success. Kids of all ages played happily and safely in the street. Impromptu bicycle races happened down the length of the block. Grills gave off delicious odors while everyone mingled, nibbled, and shared emergency stories. Late in the afternoon, someone brought out a guitar, and everyone gathered around to sing folk songs. Then Roxanne gave a short speech and gathered names for an emergency preparedness committee.

This was the beginning of two intertwining legacies that brought the whole block together into a caring community: a yearly block party, which eventually became something of a gourmet feast, and the introduction of an annual "awareness theme"—the first, of course, being emergency preparedness.

Combine these ingredients for a successful block party:

- One or two people willing to take responsibility and do the work.

- The support of a majority of the residents, and the cooperation of many of them.

- Permission from the local authorities including any necessary permits for the sale of alcoholic beverages.

- A means of blocking off the street: sawhorses, balloons, and bright ribbon, or metal traffic barriers.

- A means of clearing the space: if you want cars off the street post flyers ahead of time.

- Name tags: they seem tacky, but they really do help.

- A theme that serves as an organizing principle (for example, July Fourth).

- Voluntary donations to defray common costs.

DOG OWNERS' GROUP

"The names sound so exotic, don't they? Bichon frise, keeshond, papillon, Hungarian vizsla, schipperke. Of course what we ended up with was a Heinz 57." Ellie says this with her hearty laugh as she looks down at a creature wagging its tail frantically at her. He looks like a loaf of nine-grain bread with legs: golden brown with faint white spots, a perfect rectangle. "My son had begged for a dog since he was five, and when he turned eight I thought, Well okay; he's ready for the responsibility. Now we end up arguing about who gets to take him for a walk! We went through literally fifty possible names for this guy before we realized that we had to give him the moniker we tagged him with at the shelter. My son kept saying, 'I want the small dog! Small dog! Small dog!' So yup, his name is Small Dog. Go figure."

Ellie and four other dog "parents" are throwing a birthday party for her dog. A cake bears the message "Happy Birthday Small Dog!" in cream cheese icing. The food for the humans has been packed in the car; it contains nothing chocolate. "No chocolate ever," says Ellie, uncharacteristically solemn. "Chocolate can be deadly for dogs, so we just leave it out altogether." The drive to the local park is short and, once there, Ellie's friends set up the balloons and banners. As usual, the dog owners greet other dog owners' dogs first—the "parents" come second. Children are racing around with a collection of dogs in different sizes, shapes, and colors.

Some people think that owning a dog is a solitary experience. It certainly doesn't have to be—remember that most people respond warmly to the sight of a furry, friendly critter. The trick is to figure out how to turn this inherent friendliness into a community for yourself (and your dog). Dogs are social creatures just like people, and basically have the same needs: good food, exercise, and companionship, both with humans and with other dogs. What better way to meet these needs for both of you than to create a dog lovers' community? Here's a way to start:

- Throw a birthday party for your pet. Choose a date, time and location (with a dog you have adopted, you may have some flexibility regarding the date). For the time, choose a typical "dog walker's timetable"—the time when most people are out for the morning or afternoon walk. Your own backyard or a local park that is close by is a good choice, rather than having the party goers running through your house tipping over lamps and drinking out of the toilet.

- Advertise your desire to form a dog owners' community. There are two main ways to do this. The first is to create some invitations with construction paper cut in the shape of doghouses or bones (this is a fun activity for kids to be involved in). Then carry the invitations with you on your dog walks and hand them out to other dog owners you meet. The second way is to put up a general invitation at your veterinarian's office, pet food store, and neighborhood groomers'.

- Remember that your dog must be able and willing to socialize with people and dogs outside of your family. One advantage of handing out invitations at the park where dog owners congregate is that you can be assured that their dogs are used to playing with others.

- Dog people love talking about and being with dogs. That much seems obvious. A birthday party is a good way to start to build a community together. It's a great way to get vet recommendations or find someone to dog sit while you're away for the weekend—or get the name of a motel that'll let you bring your dog with you. You can then create a regular dog walking group for exercising the humans as well as for safety during those winter months when it gets dark early. Or you can put together a dog and human hiking jaunt by a local lake or hill. Make sure that your participants are model citizens who carry bags to scoop poop on your route.

HALCYON COMMONS

It had been a parking lot since 1933, when the Southern Pacific Redline Trains stopped running. Twenty-eight spaces down the middle of Halcyon Court, not much used, not much thought about. Then, on a lovely June day in 1992, neighbors closed the street for a block party. During the course of the revelry, someone mentioned that the neighborhood needed a park a whole lot more than a parking lot. Most folks agreed, and in that moment the Halcyon Commons Planning Committee was born.

In December of that year, the committee sent a questionnaire to everyone in the neighborhood. Ninety-four percent of those who responded endorsed the park. After a couple of architect-led design workshops and a lot of neighborhood feedback, the committee hosted another block party. This time they created a mockup of the park using house plants to stand as trees and lawn chairs and paint to mark the paths. At a second block party a few months later, volunteers actually planted twenty-one trees on Halcyon Court.

By February 1994, the committee had secured letters of endorsement from twenty-eight neighborhood groups. They'd also gotten a landscape architect to donate his time to make professional quality blueprints. All this, plus drawings from a lot of neighborhood children, were presented to the city parks and recreation commission. Result: unanimous endorsement.

In June, hundreds of neighbors with pink and white balloons filled the city council chambers when a funding vote came up. One hundred and nine thousand dollars was approved for grading, irrigation, and lighting, but the real work would be done by the neighborhood.

The next year, construction started. Bare-chested neighbors could be seen pounding sledgehammers and hefting huge chunks of asphalt into debris boxes. Everyone pitched in, planting twenty-two trees and hundreds of shrubs and bushes and sodding a lawn. Even little Gulliver Boland, age four, helped plant a flowering pear tree with his trusty plastic shovel.

Today, Halcyon Commons has benches, picnic tables, and a lovely wooden arbor. It's a place carved from asphalt and urban neglect where people can lie down on a bit of grass; where they eat lunch beneath a Japanese maple, listening to birds; where they can think and talk and recover.

You can make big changes in *your* neighborhood by following some of the strategies used by the Halcyon Commons Planning Committee. Whether you want planter boxes, sidewalk trees, speed bumps, or better lighting, you can make it happen by doing a little organizing.

- Start with a block party. Make it a potluck, but be sure to have a grill fired up and a starter course or two.

- Circulate. Try to meet everybody and ask them what they'd like to improve in the neighborhood. If you have ideas of your own, do a rough survey to see how many people agree.

- At the block party, pass around a sign-up sheet for a neighborhood improvement association.

- Establish monthly meetings and steer the group toward focusing on a single, concrete issue.

- When you've found a goal to rally around, do a written survey of your neighbors to establish the degree of agreement and enthusiasm.

- Keep the neighborhood involved with block parties or mailings, or by displaying samples or models of what you want to change.

- Get your ducks in a row. Create a formal proposal, then seek letters of support from nearby businesses and neighborhood associations. Estimate both the project's costs and the amount of volunteer labor available from your community.

- If you need government approval, create a committee to begin the lobbying effort. This may involve petitions, meetings with council members, neighborhood demonstrations, and so on.

- If you can't get the money or approval for everything you want, try to start with something small that is in your power to accomplish.

- Keep at it. Remember that any journey begins with a single step, and when enough people take that step together, it's mighty hard to stop them.

WHAT CAN KIDS DO?

Mitchell is a counselor at Kolter Middle School. He has seen teachers ready to tear their hair out over the unbridled energy and hormones kids have at that age. "The kids are loud, they're rambunctious, they're all over the place. And they seem totally self-absorbed—and sometimes they are: fascinated with their own little world like nothing else exists." He just dealt with it with good humor, generally, until about a month ago.

"Perhaps it was a stars-in-alignment thing, or maybe just coincidence, but one afternoon, I had a teacher sit in that blue chair over there and tell me her kids don't care about anything but themselves. An hour later I had this kid, Joey, sitting in this green chair over here, because he's having a tough time making friends since he transferred. And he said the same thing, that kids here don't care about anything but themselves. Interesting, huh? I just let the teacher vent, but when I heard it the second time, I asked Joey if he'd like to do a little research. I told him I'd give him extra credit for doing a survey of all his classmates. He had to ask them two questions: first, do you volunteer or help others in some way? and second, would you help out if you knew how?

Mitchell was pretty surprised when Joey came back with the results. He'd handed them out to all the homeroom classes in every grade, and because the teacher was standing there, Joey got an extremely high rate of return—which is unusual in research. "About 20 percent did some kind of helping out somewhere, but the interesting thing is that of those that didn't help out or volunteer, nine out of ten said they would if they only knew how. Some wrote at the bottom of the sheet that no one wants help from them because they're kids. We discussed it at the next staff meeting, and suddenly all these tired and burned-out teachers were getting excited and energized and looking at these kids in a whole new way."

Mitchell and the other teachers helped to implement community service projects that would give the middle-schoolers a chance to work together for the good of the larger community and to foster a sense of community within the school. The kids were asked to contribute ideas for the projects, and they accomplished this by checking the newspaper for human interest stories and problems in their town, by asking business owners and workers for their opinions, and by questioning their parents and siblings. Teachers and parents noticed that the children communicated better, were more thoughtful, asked insightful questions, and were developing decision-making and problem-solving skills. They were also nicer to each other. Well, mostly.

- Have your child make a list of what he or she enjoys doing; the list will contain skills that might be transferable to another setting.

- Help your child decide what is important to him or her. This process helps the child develop a sense of his or her values and priorities. Many kids have a sense of how they wish they could help out in the world, but most have a hard time expressing it.

- Ways to help out in a community can come through a service project in the schools, or through participation in an already existing program with a specific focus—like one that collects used eyeglasses to give to children who can't afford to buy new glasses. Putting on a garage sale whose proceeds go to a charity the child selects is another way he or she can feel a sense of contributing. Children can also volunteer in settings like hospitals, retirement homes, or wildlife rescue associations. Part of a community service project for kids could be giving out a survey to local businesses, agencies, and charitable organizations asking if they would welcome a child volunteer.

- Parents can be guides, but should know when to back off. Your role is to help your child identify a problem, set a goal, create a plan, and be responsible for seeing the commitment through to the end. Children do need the assistance of adults in order to help their community, but their efforts to be a part of the community result in increased feelings of pride and self-worth.

TEEN TUTORS

September 9th; a cartoon: Luann says to Brad, "Today's international literacy day." Brad responds, "Good. There's WAY too much litter." In the next frame, Brad says, "Oh, wait. Illiteracy is when pets get fixed to not have litters." In the last frame, Luann says, "Brad, illiteracy is when a person can't read or write. Literacy day is about helping those people. See?" She points to a newspaper article. Brad responds, "If a person can't read, how're they supposed to know that it's literacy day?"

John chuckled as he read the cartoon, and then passed the funnies to his wife, Marcia, next to him on the couch. She read the cartoon and laughed too, then handed it off to their teenage daughter, Amy, who was sitting on the rug. It was the family ritual: Sunday morning spent sprawled around the living room, sharing the newspaper. It reflected their lifelong habit of reading quietly together or aloud to each other. Amy smiled thoughtfully and then said, "You know, reading *is* great." Marcia chimed in with, "Helpful too. I wonder if there's something that we can do to help others improve their reading skills?"

Amy went on the Internet and discovered that, according to the 1993 National Adult Literacy Survey (NALS), more than 40 million Americans are functionally illiterate. *Functional literacy* is defined as a range of tools that help people to help themselves, because these days, reading is not just an end in itself; it's a means to a better quality of life. "Damn," thought Amy. "My mom was right." That's how RIGHT (Reading Is Great, Helpful Too) got started.

John and Marcia had a cadre of friends, couples who had met at a cooperative nursery school many years earlier. Their kids were all teenagers now, and the parents were always trying to figure out ways to get the kids involved in community projects. A literacy campaign of teens-tutoring-kids seemed to fit the bill. Marcia invited everyone over for a potluck dessert the following Wednesday evening. John made brownies, and remembered to invite Marian, the head librarian of the local library.

As it turned out, Marian had been thinking about a literacy project for a while. She had already contacted a group called Literacy Volunteers of America, which would provide training materials. What they really needed now were volunteers. The parents started brainstorming. One promising idea was to bribe their kids by trading off regular chores for tutoring time. Another idea was that the teens could earn "credits" by tutoring. The credits could be cashed in for later curfew times or use of the family car. Amy offered to have a slumber party with her girlfriends. The idea was to stay up all night taking turns reading from trashy novels—then signing up the girls to be tutors.

After a couple of weeks, a buzz started going around the high school that an elite "tutoring team" had been formed. And each week thirty elementary students were selected by their teachers to meet with their tutors, who were already becoming role models and friends.

If you're thinking of starting a literacy project involving teenagers:

- ⊚ Check out the National Institute for Literacy Web site at: http://www.nifl.gov. Here you'll find FAQs and links to programs and publications.

- ⊚ Contact your local head librarian. He or she may have a literary program already in the works that your group can hook into.

- ⊚ To motivate teens, consider the use of a reward system in the beginning. Later, the inherent rewards of helping and befriending the younger kids will keep them coming back for more.

- ⊚ To connect teens who want to tutor with younger children who need help. Work with the faculty and administration of both the high school and a middle or elementary school. Psychologists or counselors on the faculty can help make the most appropriate matches.

ON THE ROAD READING GROUP

Louisa May Alcott said, "Good books, like good friends, are few and chosen; the more select, the more enjoyable."

When Jeanne was in college she read George Eliot's novels along with her roommate, who was taking a class on the author. "I had this fantasy of reading Eliot while traipsing across the English countryside, dressed in a very warm sweater while pretending to be a beautiful heiress." She grins and pours another cup of coffee for one of her reading group buddies.

"Yeah," says Pat. "My fantasy was to hang out in New England for a month reading everything John Cheever ever wrote. Sipping a martini from one hand and carrying a tennis racket in the other. It seems like most of us had that wish, to read an author while soaking in the atmosphere that the writer was describing on paper. To see the landmarks that were important to their stories—the small towns, the evocative landscapes." The six other women in the group nod in excited sympathy.

"I think that's why we wanted to go beyond the traditional reading group, to get out there on the road. We've been down to Monterey and read and digested Steinbeck. Last year the big trip was to New York, where we read and explored the haunts of Edith Wharton, Edgar Allan Poe, and Dorothy Parker.

"This year we're going to Tuscany! It was the inspiration for so many authors—Forster, D. H. Lawrence, and Henry James, as well as Michael Ondaatje."

If you want to start an "on the road" reading group, remember that unless you are retired or independently wealthy, you won't be able to travel all the time. But having a reading group that meets regularly throughout the year and plans for two trips a year is manageable for most.

- Group size is important; eight to ten members is small enough so that everyone gets a chance to talk but large enough to adapt to members' occasional absences.

- Decide how to make your book selections. Do you want to focus on biographies or other nonfiction? Mysteries? Foreign authors?

- Appoint the most organized person (or people) to keep track of what's been read and what will be read in future, send reminders of upcoming meetings, have a host and snack schedule, and, if necessary, contact a local bookstore to have enough copies in stock of the upcoming books. Someone will also need to make group flight and/or hotel reservations and scout out the important literary landmarks your group will want to visit.

- Think about whether or not your group wants a professional leader. This person might come from your library or a bookstore; he or she can help your group pick books and create questions for discussion. If you do without a leader, you can get reading group guides from various publisher and bookstore sites on the Web, like Amazon or Vintage. You can also have a member research an author's background and biographical details.

- Some reading groups invite authors or other experts to give talks. If your group loves Patricia Cornwell, you might contact a medical examiner to speak.

- Do some research on local authors. This is the easiest and least expensive way to start the "on the road" aspect of the group. Plan a day trip to see streets, bars, and restaurants that are mentioned in their books, or visit a collection that's kept in their honor, like the Henry Miller Memorial Library in Big Sur, California.

- Plan a more ambitious trip well in advance. You will want your group to read several books by the author who wrote about a particular locale, or works by a collection of authors who were influenced by a particular region. Discover museums, walking tours, or local talks devoted to that author. Some towns have cottage industries built around their famous native sons or daughters and can provide a unique immersion experience.

A WRITING GROUP

The reclusive J. D. Salinger once granted a rare interview to a young writer. What's the secret, the young man asked, to an achievement like *Catcher in the Rye* or *Franny and Zooey*? There is no secret, Salinger said. You just have to write. Every day. Whether you want to or not. Whether it's crap or not. Whether anyone reads it or not. Just write.

But there *is* a secret, and every writer knows about it. It's motivation: where do you find the drive to write every day? How do you keep going back to your desk and struggling with the words? It's hard work. But worse, it's lonely work. There's no one to help or support you while you duke it out with a blank page.

George Lorimer once said that "Writing is like religion. Everyone who feels the call must work out his own salvation." One means to salvation is the writing group: supportive, interested people who regularly listen to each other's work. It motivates you to keep scribbling, because you're looking forward to reading it aloud to the group and hearing what they think about it.

Some years ago, Matt started a weekly poetry group for just this purpose. He began by signing up some friends who were poets. Then he ran an ad for the group in *Poetry Flash*, a free newspaper that caters to serious writers. Finally, he put signs up in the English departments of some local colleges. The group met Thursday nights in Matt's living room.

The sessions were lively: the members brought strong, often moving work—and lots of opinions. To keep things constructive, it was agreed that feedback would consist of a comment on the thing you liked most about a poem, balanced by one suggestion for change. People didn't always stay with this structure, but everyone made an effort to offer balanced feedback and find at least one positive thing to say.

For Matt and many in the group, Thursday night functioned as a strong incentive to finish a piece, or at least to get enough done that there was something to read. But staying focused was just one dividend. Because group members had a wide variety of writing styles and interests, there was a cross-fertilization effect: they were learning from each other, getting inspired by each other, taking new risks with words.

There is an immediacy that comes from sharing your writing, particularly poetry. Friendships form, and these friends know each other—emotionally and intellectually—in ways few people do. They feel seen, because their writing is a window for others to look through; it opens places that would otherwise remain hidden. Matt's group is gone now, but he still has three good friends that came from it. And they still share their work.

If you want to start a writing group, we suggest the following:

- Advertise at coffeehouses and other venues where writers congregate. Put up signs on university kiosks and in English departments. Put notices in local writing or poetry magazines. Make announcements at open mic poetry readings.

- Keep to a structure: start and end on time and limit people to no more than eight to ten minutes of reading. Encourage balanced feedback, and kick people out of the group who are harsh or cruel—they'll ruin it for everyone else.

- Weekly meetings are the best means to reinforce daily writing.

- Encourage everyone to participate, even if they aren't up to the skill level of some others. Emphasize that the group's purpose is support, not biting literary criticism.

- Whether your group focuses on poetry or prose, it helps if members pass out copies of their work before they read it aloud. Seeing it on the page makes for better feedback.

LANGUAGE GROUP

"I hated that language requirement in high school. The teacher made it so dry and boring that it had nothing whatever to do with the real world. I would overhear people speaking Spanish on the bus or in a restaurant and I'd catch a word or two that I recognized but no more. I live in an area that has a high population of Spanish speakers and I couldn't communicate with any of them. I just think that's sad, and a waste."

Mary's desire for connection with others in her community drove her to develop her own community in order to learn to speak Spanish. "As an adult I realized that the best way to start was to go back to the classroom again. But I had also figured out that the way to connect was beyond the confines of a Spanish textbook, filling in the blanks of exercise numero cuatro. I knew I would feel more comfortable, at least at the beginning, taking some risks by practicing with other English speakers who were struggling just like me. So part of the point of my taking the class was to put together a group for outside of class."

Approaching others in the class initially felt difficult, but Mary was surprised by the response. Five out of the twenty students were interested enough to meet for coffee after class and talk about what they would wish to get out of a language group. "We all wanted Spanish-speaking people to know that we were trying to communicate on their terms, not expecting others to always adapt to us." They identified three areas of communication in any language: understanding the language spoken by others, being able to speak it themselves, and being able to read the language. The group of five made a list of activities that would help them in these areas. Once a month they went to a neighborhood grocery store and, supporting each other with hints and reminders, bought food for a dinner that they then cooked together. They made every effort to restrict themselves to asking for items only in Spanish.

To cook dinner, they translated recipe directions into Spanish. After a little food and good Spanish wine, they would take turns reading aloud from a Spanish novel, or watch a movie they had rented and discover how much they could understand without reading the subtitles. They became rather addicted to the Spanish soaps on television.

Right now Mary is taking salsa lessons with her group twice a month; they speak English only as a last resort. Eventually they hope to have friendships they can conduct in Spanish. The world is opening up more each week.

- Take a class in your language of choice. It helps give a focus to your studying as well as offering a population of people who might be interested in starting a group.

- Identify what goals the group has. The focus of Mary's group was learning to communicate about everyday experiences: shopping for dinner, following directions, ordering in restaurants.

- If you live in a good-sized city, it is likely that there are enclaves of people from various parts of the world. Read your local newspaper or use the Internet to discover what these groups are and where they congregate.

- Ask yourselves what activities your group can do to practice the language you wish to learn. In Mary's city there was a large Spanish-speaking population, so it was easy for her to find a grocery store to practice her skills in. If there are no international shops or restaurants in your area, newspaper kiosks are great places to get newspapers and magazines in other languages. You can improve your vocabulary and your knowledge of current events at the same time. If your bookstore doesn't have books in other languages, your public library might.

- The best way to learn is to practice frequently. Meet frequently, and keep the emphasis on fun rather than work. Once the group feels more confident, be open to making friends with native speakers and including them in your get-togethers.

A MOVEABLE FEAST

Peter loved to cook. In fact he had even self-published a small cookbook dedicated to his children. And now, two years after his divorce, he stood alone in his remodeled gourmet kitchen—butcher block and granite surfaces, a downdraft cooktop with an indoor grill, and an oven with a built-in rotisserie—with no one to cook for.

He decided to join a cooking class. He could always pick up a few new tips, but his real reason was to meet other people who enjoyed cooking and eating. The local gourmet food shop was offering a series of three-hour classes featuring the cuisines of different countries. Peter chose the French class, which focused on hors d'oeuvres.

Before going to the class, Peter prepared a flyer that he hoped to distribute to his classmates. The flyer requested that all interested people who wanted to practice what they had learned contact him by telephone or e-mail. The class instructor readily agreed to the flyer being circulated after the class was over. Peter also posted the flyers on the bulletin board.

Within a week, he had six responses from interested amateur chefs. (Luckily, all of them had e-mail, so communication was made easy.) A date two weeks later was set for an hors d'oeuvres and cocktail gathering at Peter's house. All participants were to bring either something they had prepared at home or the ingredients necessary to cook in Peter's kitchen. Peter made brochettes ris de veau (the recipe is below) on the indoor grill while the others gathered around and sipped on their cocktails. Everyone enjoyed noshing and sharing food and recipes.

Emboldened by the success of that first evening, Peter decided to try something different a few months later. This time, it was a class on Parisian cooking that caught his eye. Again he prepared flyers; however, this time he proposed a moveable feast with a theme of French cuisine. A moveable feast is a meal where each course is served at a different participant's home, so the party literally moves from place to place throughout the evening. The ideal situation for a moveable feast is to gather several people living in the same neighborhood, condo complex, or apartment building. This way the group can walk from place to place together.

Peter got some responses from the cooking students in that class; he also contacted members of the hors d'oeuvres group. Again, several people, including couples, were willing to sign up for the event. Unfortunately, the group was spread out geographically, so they formed carpools. Since wine and cocktails were being served, each car had a designated driver for the evening.

To simplify things, Peter proposed a four course menu: hors d'oeuvres, soup and salad, main course, and dessert and coffee. Peter signed up to make a coq au vin for the main course. He prepared it ahead of time and kept it hot in a Crockpot so that it was ready to eat when he and the rest of the group arrived at his house.

Peter kept exploring different ethnic cuisines using the same strategy. Eventually, a congenial group was established. They have moveable feasts four times a year, taking turns preparing the main course.

Tips for initiating a moveable feast:

◉ Look for places where other people who like to cook hang out (e.g., cooking classes), and advertise or hang out there.

◉ When planning a moveable feast, schedule no more than three to four courses. Plan on a three-hour evening, allowing about forty-five minutes at each stop.

◉ If both drinking and driving are going to be involved, have a designated driver for each vehicle.

Brochettes ris de veau: Parboil calf sweetbreads and cut them into square pieces. Put them on metal skewers, alternating with cubes of lean ham and sliced, cooked mushrooms. Brush the brochettes with melted butter, roll in fine bread crumbs, and grill over moderate heat.

GAMES NIGHT

The Ohlone tribe of Native Americans were famous for their love of games: racing games, dice games, elaborately staged dance competitions, plus a game with a puck and sticks that was very much like cricket. They were so competitive that they'd fight ruthlessly to win, totally engrossed in the struggle.

But when the game was over, members of the Ohlone tribe were among the most harmonious and tightly knit of any Native American group. They were also an amazingly relaxed and easygoing people—maybe because they got to act out all their feelings of aggression inside a structured game.

In our culture, people eat together and they drink together, but only rarely do they play together—a *real* game, with winners and losers, that's completely focused on the battle. We are less for it: less relaxed, less close.

The French philosopher Blaise Pascal wrote that the sole purpose of any game is the will to diversion, an effort to distract ourselves from the grim realities of life. He was right. And although he saw diversion as a kind of vice, a pathological escape, it serves the same vital purpose for us now that it did for the Ohlone tribe. It focuses us, and helps us let go of everything else.

Jeremy, a computer repairman in Atlanta, loved board games but could never get any of his buddies interested. So he decided to start a games club. He put an ad in the newsletter of a large singles organization in Atlanta. He also photocopied some flyers and gave them out to customers who seemed the type to be interested. He arranged that everyone would gather in the meeting hall of a local library, which was free to nonprofit groups.

The games Jeremy started with were backgammon, Scrabble, Parcheesi, and the old Parker Brothers games Risk and Monopoly. The first night, seven men and one woman showed up. Jeremy provided complimentary soft drinks and chips and dip while great contests were waged.

Over succeeding weeks, Jeremy kept advertising, deliberately giving more flyers to women to improve the gender balance. Attendance varied, but eventually he got a steady core group of between six and twelve. Risk and Monopoly fell by the boards, as it were, because most of the group seemed to prefer either Scrabble or backgammon. The gender ratio continued to be skewed, but there were two or three women who came frequently.

Jeremy's games group flourished for a number of years. It was fertile ground for the growth of friendships. The "game nuts," as they called themselves, often did other things together—movies, ski trips, fishing trips. And when Jeremy needed an appendectomy, the game nuts were all over his hospital room, forcing the poor man to play backgammon before the anesthetic had completely worn off. "Only way I can beat him," one of them said.

If you'd like to create your own games club, we suggest:

- Ads in laundries, coffeehouses, ice cream shops, and community and singles newsletters. You can also put flyers on kiosks at local colleges. Keep advertising after the club starts, because a lot of people will try it once or twice and drop out.

- Screen the people who call to make sure they sound reasonable and are interested in the games you want to play.

- Meet in a public place initially.

- Start with a wide variety of games, then be flexible as you learn what people want to play.

- Serve soft drinks and hors d'oeuvres. Eventually club members can take turns bringing them.

- Meet monthly, or at most every two weeks.

THE BBC
(BOULDER BEER COLLECTIVE)

It was a lazy summer afternoon in Boulder, Colorado. Bert was sitting in his backyard, drinking a lonely beer and wondering how to make his life better. In a flash of insight, the amazingly simple answer came to him. Bert wanted more beer, and some friends to share it with. "How about," he thought to himself, "gathering a group of beer drinkers together to MAKE OUR OWN BEER?"

The first step was to gather information. Since this story happened long before the Internet was popular, Bert went to the public library, where he found a book on beer making in section 641.2 B, *Brewing Quality Beers: The Home Brewer's Essential Guidebook* by Byron Burch. By searching through the yellow pages, he located a beer and wine making supply store just fifteen minutes from his house. There he found the classic, *The Complete Handbook of Home Brewing*, by Dave Miller.

Next, Bert called his best friend Harry and told him about his idea. Harry was very receptive. He had helped his father make home brew as a child and remembered the basic processes. He also said that he knew several other guys he'd be willing to call. These guys also knew a couple of other guys, and two weeks later the first meeting of the BBC (Boulder Beer Collective) was held in Bert's backyard.

Bert called the meeting to order with a beer toast to the new enterprise. Next, Bert and Harry were elected cobraumeisters by acclamation, and Bert proceeded with the agenda.

The first item was cash commitment. Bert figured that they needed about $200 to get started. This would pay for basic supplies, such as malt, hops, a primary fermenter (a brand-new plastic garbage can), air locks (to prevent harmful bacteria from entering while allowing gas to escape), a hydrometer (to measure the specific gravity of the beer, which allows you to predict its alcohol content), plastic tubes, a glass carboy (a five-gallon water cooler bottle), and a bottle capper. Since there were eight guys, this came to only $25 each; this was acceptable to the group.

The second agenda item was finding a location for brewing and storage. Bert said that if the rest of the guys would help him move stuff, he was willing to clear out the space by the back wall of his garage for the project. Everyone agreed, and Jack offered his pickup truck to haul stuff to the dump.

Now the group discussed what kind of beer to make for their first project. Several of the members of the group suggested steam beer. Bert consulted his *Complete Handbook of Home Brewing* and was surprised to find a recipe (page 224) that seemed easy to follow. The book also informed him that steam beer sometimes explodes ordinary beer bottles, but that champagne bottles are strong enough and can be capped like beer bottles. Charlie volunteered time at the local recycling center; he figured he could divert enough champagne bottles for this project.

Two weeks later, all the supplies were assembled, and the BBC got to work washing and sterilizing the equipment using a ready-made compound consisting of trisodium phosphate and chlorine. The actual brewing part was easy, with everyone reading and double checking the procedure from the book. The group kept a "brewer's log" to provide a reliable record of the recipes they used and procedures followed.

The following week, the group met again and began the bottling process, carefully washing and sterilizing the champagne bottles that Charlie had supplied. After all the bottles were filled and capped, the toughest part of the process began—waiting. Some things just can't be hurried.

Finally, a month later, the big day arrived. Bert cautiously uncapped the first carefully chilled bottle and poured some beer into his glass. He paused to admire the creamy head, and took a sip. Then, with a smile, he filled everyone else's glass. Amazingly, it was good. Murmurs of approval filled the air, and someone said, "I think this is the beginning of a beautiful friendship."

To start a successful beer making group:

◉ Though books and trial-and-error can get you started, having someone with a minimal amount of experience with the fermentation process minimizes error and frustration.

- Everything most be kept scrupulously clean. A good home-brewing book will give you good cleaning advice.

- As beer drinkers like to say, "It's the water." Be sure to use chlorine-free water. It's easiest to use a local pure bottled spring water in making beer, but you can also remove the chlorine and some minerals from tap water by boiling it. Let it cool completely before using it.

- Keep a careful log of *exactly* what you do This will help you figure out what went wrong if you get a bad batch.

- Have patience. . . .

KNIT 1, PURL 2

When Martha was a child, her grandmother lived with her and her parents for about five years before moving into a retirement community in southern California. What Martha remembers best is the Sunday afternoon knitting bee that her grandmother held with her friends. She recalls the easy flow of conversation, the smell of fresh coffee cake, and the endless cups of tea. Her grandmother was the first to put a crochet hook and a ball of pale blue yarn in her small hands. There was always some kind of project in her grandmother's large crafts basket, and usually there were three or four.

"I grew up in an era when the emphasis was on doing well financially and being satisfied in your career, not on the value of anything handmade. I could just kick myself now," says Martha, her eyes filling with tears momentarily. "I had no idea what I had. I always wanted store-bought things. In elementary school I even hid the things my grandmother made. It makes me ashamed that I didn't value her and the beautiful things she created with her own hands. I told her on the phone a while back that I had taken up knitting, as a kind of stress buster. She said that was wonderful but that knitting in the company of others, and knitting for others, would bring me much more. I tried to tell her how sorry I am that I didn't appreciate the intricate sweaters and the afghans and the socks, but she just kind of stopped me. She gets to the heart of things pretty fast. 'Well, now you know better, Martie. So go do something with it. You have my address down here. Send me something you've made when you're done.' So I'm doing it, partly to dump the guilt of being such an ungrateful kid, but partly because I feel like I've discovered something I can do that has no deadline, lets me use my hands, and is, well, beautiful. I love the positive feedback I get from the people I knit with."

Martha particularly likes having a hobby that is entirely portable and can be taken up at the drop of a hat. "And we're working on hats now," she says with a grin, "lots of them." One of Martha's current projects, and one she does with a group of six other people, is knitting caps for women who have had radiation treatment for cancer. A large basket sits on the floor of her local knit shop and the knitters sit around a long oak table, each working on a bright and colorful hat that will be added to the basket. Every month, a new batch is taken over to the local cancer care center and distributed for free. Martha also spends Sunday afternoons knitting with some of the same people, working on sweaters with cables from Rowan tweed yarns, scarves from soft chenille, and children's vests with complicated patterns of flowers or cars. They have an easy flow of talk (and of course cake and many cups of tea). And Martha carries her knitting bag with her wherever she goes and always has a project going, just like her grandmother.

- Visit a few knitting stores to find personnel who are friendly and helpful. The presence of a large table with people sitting and knitting on their own is a good sign that the owner likes patrons to drop by to knit a few rows and chat. Avoid shops where the point is solely to sell you more yarn and get you out the door.

- Invite people you have met at the knit shop over to work on their projects some weekend afternoon. Knitting in a group is especially helpful if you make a mistake, since someone is likely to provide a solution—or at least to provide support if you have to go through the trauma of ripping out a section you just finished. Remember to be very careful with food and beverages; keep them away from the yarn. Cats and exploring toddlers should also be kept at a distance from all knitting projects.

- Think of some projects that others in your group might wish to donate time and energy for. Many people in need would love a beautiful hat, muffler, or socks. Adopting a school and knitting children's mittens is another idea. One group developed a small business knitting tiny sweaters the size of a pack of cards and selling them as gift decorations. The possibilities are endless.

JENNY'S MOVIE CLUB

"I thought that movie had all the interest of a jar of pennies."

"Don't go overboard with your praise, Bill."

"The movie can't make up its mind what it is." Bill took another spoonful of an overflowing bowl of Fenton's ice cream. "Is it comedy, romance, drama? It just keeps wobbling back and forth and settles nowhere."

Jenny pointed her spoon at him. "Tell me you didn't love it when John Turturro threw his harebrained mother out the window. That's one of the most satisfying moments I've ever had at the movies."

"Right." Gary was wiping a huge gob of chocolate off his shirt. "Turturro makes a great madman. But I thought Jodie Foster didn't stretch herself much in the movie. She kind of walked through it."

"I thought she looked really scared when Turturro was chasing her in the sub-way—that was good," Lucy chimed in from a second table.

"What about Tim Robbins, the reluctant hero?" Beth wanted to know.

"He looks too much like Dobie Gillis to take seriously, I'm sorry." Annette vainly tried to get the waiter's attention. "But what I liked was how he explained his commit-ment to civil rights—the love of justice came straight out of his love for his father."

And so the conversation continued in the little group at two shoved-together tables in a crowded ice cream parlor. They meet together once a month to view a first-run movie, then enjoy a critical discussion afterward over dessert. Through the years they've become friends. But they were complete strangers when Movie of the Month Club started back in 1990.

It was Jenny's idea. She's a complete movie nut who sees most of the new films. "I got sick of going to movies with people who couldn't or didn't want to talk about them," Jenny says. "It was trenchant analysis like 'That was cool' or "Bummer movie, man.' I'd be talking about things like camera angle, length of take, or McGuffins, and they'd be going, 'Whatever.'"

Jenny made an announcement to everyone at work and put an ad for her group in *Shipmates*, the newsletter for a large Presbyterian singles organization. People came and went for the first six months, but eventually Movie of the Month Club gelled at about ten regular members.

The current system is that Jenny nominates five first-run movies each month, and the group votes via e-mail for the one they most want to see. Jenny then selects a convenient theater and the after-movie dessert location—an ice cream parlor, late night coffee shop, or someone's house. As a bonus, Jenny, Annette, and Lucy have become great friends, and often get together for dinner before the film.

If you'd like to start your own movie club, we'd suggest the following:

- Start with a nucleus of interested friends. Then put the word out at work. If you still need more people, put an ad in a singles newsletter, or even the classifieds of a neighborhood paper. Sometimes a local theater will be willing to put up a small sign advertising the group.

- Try to get a minimum of eight to ten people. Not everyone shows up each month, and there will inevitably be dropouts. Keep up the advertising during the first few months until the group gels.

- Democracy is usually preferrable to autocracy. Set up a system for the club to vote on which films to see.

- Encourage variety. Some movie clubs rotate the genre they'll see—foreign, comedy, adventure, indie features, and so on.

- Always prearrange a meeting place after the film. In the beginning, this will probably be restaurants where you can order coffee and dessert. Later, as group cohesion builds, you can rotate after-movie dessert at different people's homes.

- Encourage civility in the discussion. People who are contemptuous of others' views simply shouldn't get invited the next month.

- Try expanding your activities—see if you can drum up interest in plays, music, cultural events, and so on. Subgroups of the club may meet to enjoy these alternative events.

GRASSROOTS: FROM THE GROUND UP

What if you care very deeply about an issue that no one seems to know much about? What if others know about it but they seem to believe that they can't change anything because it's just too big a problem to handle or "it's always been done that way"? Are you the lone voice in the wilderness? Here are two grassroots organizations, both over a century old, that began as the result of individual passion, concern, and dedication, and are now among American society's most revered institutions.

The Sierra Club

John Muir discovered the Sierra Nevada in 1868 on his way to study botany in the Amazon, and he pretty much never left. Transformed by the astounding beauty of the wilderness that he saw in Yosemite, he stayed on, and twenty-eight years later, in 1892, he founded the Sierra Club. Muir combined his personal enthusiasm with that of influential people and of a group from the University of California to form the fledgling organization. The hallmarks of the Sierra Club are its passionate environmentalism, its political activism, and its impressive ability to shape American environmental policy, altering big corporations' patterns of environmental exploitation. With its three main purposes—recreational, educational, and conservationist—the Sierra Club eventually expanded beyond the Sierras into preserving wildlife and wilderness across the nation. Recently, the Sierra Club helped stall DuPont's plans to strip-mine Trail Ridge in southern Georgia, plans which would have had grave consequences for air and water quality, wildlife, and vegetation.

The American Red Cross

Clara Barton used her experience as a relief worker in the Franco-Prussian War to convince the United States to sign the Geneva conventions. She founded the American

Association of the Red Cross in 1881. Her particular efforts were in organizing and managing volunteers to assist with the victims of disasters, whether fire, flood, or famine. In the late 1800s, Red Cross volunteers provided food and clothing to the victims of Michigan forest fires, and provided shelter and medical assistance to flood victims of the Ohio and Mississippi rivers as well as of the Johnstown, Pennsylvania flood. More recently, the Red Cross was instrumental in providing care and assistance to the victims of September 11th, 2001.

- What are you passionate about? What need do you believe is unmet? What wrong needs to be righted? Create your own mission statement about what the problem is and what it takes to correct it.

- Do some research to locate an existing group or person who is interested in achieving the same goals, and get in touch with that person or group. Two (or two hundred) heads are better than one.

- Where can you get the word out, and how? Who is most likely to be interested and supportive? For example, if you are concerned about the possible closing of a local health clinic that serves low income people, try bulletin boards at hospitals and schools. Does your area have a free neighborhood newspaper where you might advertise to contact those most affected by the issue? Internet listservs can be a rich source of contacts, especially for concerns that have a wider than local scope.

- Go for the support of the people with power. Both John Muir and Clara Barton did this, and effected wide-reaching change. Most often, this will mean your local city or state government, but it also might be someone on a corporate or nonprofit board of directors or in a neighborhood association.

- Use the media to get the word out. Local radio and television stations and neighborhood or city papers might interview you or write a feature article on your cause. When pitching to the media, and when you're interviewed, be clear about what the problem is, what the consequences of inaction will be, who you are, and what you want (volunteers, money, legislative change).

⊙ Do you want petitions signed? Making your group's presence felt at health or crafts fairs and holiday festivals can get the word out about your group, provide information and education to the community, and result in lots of signatures. Be aware that you may need a permit to set up sidewalk tables in your city.

STOP POLLUTION

Tom Lehrer was singing a song (aptly titled "Pollution"), which included the line, "The breakfast garbage that you throw in the Bay, they drink at lunch in San Jose." That was it. Miguel lived in San Jose, and hearing that line was the last bit of motivation that he needed. He decided then and there that it was time to do something on the local level to stop pollution.

Thinking back to his youth in the barrio, he remembered that the biggest polluters, the factories with tall smokestacks billowing toxic fumes, always seemed to be located near where he and his friends and family lived. He was now a senior at San Jose State, and he wondered how accurate these memories were. He decided to do some research.

Sure enough, he discovered that not only in San Jose but nationwide, toxic waste sites and polluted air and water are disproportionately found in low-income neighborhoods. He found out that 437 counties in the country contain LULUs—locally unwanted land use sites, or locations close to an environmental hazard like a smelter or a refinery. Those 437 counties are home to 65 percent of African Americans and 80 percent of Hispanics nationwide. He also discovered that his parents' home was in a LULU.

Inspired by the work of Hazel Johnson, who founded People for Community Recovery (PCR) on Chicago's South Side, Miguel decided to start a grassroots, community-based organization. And so CAUSA (Comunidades Asambleades Unidas para un Sostenible Ambiente) was born. The goals of the organization were to build local awareness of environmental justice issues and to develop and implement strategies to reduce the health threats to residents of the affected communities. Miguel wrote a grant proposal and received funding from the National Institute of Environmental Health Science (NIEHS).

The actual work began when Miguel and a few friends from college started knocking on neighbors' doors and asking them to fill out health surveys. Not surprisingly, they discovered alarming patterns of severe health problems. Asthma, skin rashes, liver problems, and cancer all occurred at higher than average rates.

Miguel summarized the findings in a flyer, which he distributed widely. A local meeting was held in the public library to discuss these findings. This was the beginning of an organizing campaign to get the neighborhood cleaned up. Committees comprising both CAUSA members and local residents were formed to put pressure on corporate polluters and on city and state officials to make them aware of and accountable for their actions. As the organization developed further research about specific polluters, one group began to write letters to the editor and articles for the local newspapers.

CAUSA became a living entity as members worked together, ate together, argued, and strategized. They produced a series of newsletters and distributed them door to door. Among their other tactics were organizing marches and rallies, picketing the polluters' plants and holding local speaking tours and press conferences. One of their most effective and popular strategies was a bilingual street theater troupe which used ten-foot-tall puppets and a mariachi band to attract large crowds.

Their actions brought real and tangible results, notably the closing, cleanup, and relocation of a glass recycling plant (escaping glass dust had been causing respiratory problems in the community). Other achievements included forcing the EPA to close down an incinerator and successfully pressuring the city not to renew the conditional use permit for a plant that produced methyl bromide. Both of these facilities were located adjacent to homes where multigenerational families lived and where children played in contaminated backyards.

When organizing your community around an issue like pollution, consider the following:

- Start with people you know.

- Gather information by going door to door.

- Educate the community and work to mobilize it into action.

- Use local resources, including volunteers, public facilities, and existing community groups.

- Write a grant proposal to try to get outside funding.

MENTORING THE GAYLON WAY

Gaylon Logan had a vision. Literally. Lying in his bunk in jail, he had a dream in which he saw two roads. One road led to crime, drugs, and early death. The other led to a place where he had built something for himself and his community.

Some time later, Gaylon was hired as a playground attendant. This was at a grade school in Hunter's Point, a San Francisco neighborhood so tough that nearly every family has been touched by the violence on the street. Children grow up terrorized. And many learn, in time, to do some terrorizing themselves.

Gaylon now saw, quite clearly, exactly where that second road would lead. He founded an after-school mentoring program called Athletic and Academic Olympics. Via advertising and a lot of word-of-mouth proselytizing, Gaylon built a volunteer network of successful black community leaders who wanted to help: sportspeople, businesspeople, folks with specific skills and accomplishments.

The volunteers met in groups to learn about and prepare themselves for mentoring roles. Then they were assigned to various afternoon and evening programs. Athletic and Academic Olympics is now a big deal. Powered by Gaylon's volunteers, it tutors kids for success both on the playing field and in the classroom. Every six months, there's an "Olympic" event where 120 kids compete using words and numbers, arms and legs.

The Athletic and Academic Olympics is just one of many mentoring programs Gaylon has inaugurated. His volunteers, for example, are having extraordinary success with Life Skills in America. This program teaches kids how to budget and balance a checkbook, how to prioritize rent and food and recreation. It's all done with Monopoly money, but the children are acquiring vital survival skills from volunteers with track records in the world of business and finance.

Gaylon's programs are focused on the grammar school level. But lots of kids have been with him for years, and some of these are in his Speakers' Bureau. Here, volunteers with speech-making skills teach children how to talk in front of groups, such as the Lions' Club, the Kiwanis, and downtown business associations, to let the world know there's something new going down in Hunter's Point.

Starting your own community mentoring program might involve some of the following steps:

- Identify a single school to start with. Build a relationship with the principal and key staff.

- The hook is athletics, so advertise in community papers for volunteers who can teach desired athletic skills. But also seek volunteers who can tutor kids in math and verbal skills. Volunteers must be screened for their capacity to relate to children. Nerdy, weird, and socially awkward volunteers are going to turn kids off and ruin the program's reputation. The whole point is to get mentors the kids can look up to.

- From the beginning, link athletics and academics: kids aren't allowed to do one without working hard at the other.

- Schedule regular competitions in both the athletic and academic programs. Perhaps the best way to do this is to have the kids compete with their own previous records, not with each other; for example, doing your times tables faster with fewer errors than in the last competition, or running a 220-yard race to beat your previous best time.

RECLAIMING THE PARK

Juneteenth. The oldest known celebration of the ending of slavery dates back to June 19, 1865. That's when Union soldiers, led by Major General Gordon Granger, arrived in Galveston, Texas with the news that those enslaved were now free (two and a half years after the Emancipation Proclamation had become official, on January 1st, 1863). Juneteenth became an official state holiday in Texas in 1980. Observances usually focus on self-improvement; the celebration itself, however, is physically centered around a huge barbecue pit.

The annual Juneteenth party in the community of Roebuck, Cincinnati, was noisily underway. But this time there was more in the air than just the smoky aroma of barbecued ribs and Louisiana hot links. People in the neighborhood were fed up with the drug addicts and drunks who had taken over the corner park, and were determined to reclaim it for their children.

K'Meesha, K.M. to her friends, and a widowed single mother of twins, was the most determined of all. It was her daughter who had dug up the first needle in the sandbox. Carrying it precariously (but safely, praise Allah) on her little shovel, K'Alisha showed her mother what she had found. K'Alyx followed not far behind with some blood-stained cotton balls carefully balanced on her own shovel. Residents had been complaining for years about how the park had gotten run down and had become a haven for undesirable activity. Drunks sleeping it off surrounded by broken bottles was bad enough, but the twins' discovery was the last straw. Not surprisingly, K.M. became the galvanizing force in organizing the Take Back the Park committee.

The committee devised a simple three-point plan. The first step was to hold the annual Juneteenth celebration in the park this year. This would serve to highlight the deplorable conditions. The next step was to organize the community into action. K.M. got the ball rolling with a speech carefully timed for that moment when people had their mouths full but weren't comatose yet. She had volunteers circulate through the crowd with sign-up sheets for the big cleanup weekend, a month away. She also contacted other local organizations such as the PTA, Planned Parenthood, the Roebuck Neighborhood Association, the Senior Circle, and the local branch of the VFW.

The following month, at 8 A.M. on a Saturday morning, forty-five community members, young and old, converged on the park. Armed with gloves, shovels, rakes, pruning saws, and other implements, they got to work. The neighborhood association had arranged for a large Dumpster, and the parks department sent over a chipper to convert the brush and branches into mulch. By 3 P.M. Sunday, the difference was striking. Hiding areas were gone. There was not a glint of glass anywhere. Evidence abounded of freshly planted wildflowers. All agreed it was a good thing that K.M. had brought a Polaroid camera to take before and after pictures.

The final piece of the plan involved the police department. It began with the formation of a watchdog group from the community who agreed to be vigilant and to report all suspicious activity and drinking in the park (see Neighborhood Watch). The police established a zero tolerance policy for alcohol and drugs in the park, and assigned police cruisers to do frequent drive-bys, using searchlights at night.

The neighborhood association felt so good about the change in the park that they allocated funds to upgrade the playground. The upgraded area would be fenced off with redwood pickets. Inside, "sliding ponds" (slide-upons), teeter-totters, and a rubber tire maze would be nestled in redwood bark mulch, for safety. And of course there would be a new sandbox with carefully sifted sparkling white sand. K.M.'s twins, with brand-new shovels, would soon play safely and contentedly.

To reclaim a local park:

- Get local people involved, and encourage them to use the park for community activities.

- Organize the community to remove the trash—and, most important of all, to remove potential hiding places.

- Establish a partnership with the local police department to curtail illegal activity.

ORGANIZING YOUR APARTMENT BUILDING

The neighborhood itself seemed like it had given up, thrown in the towel, ceased to battle against the inevitable downward pull of garbage, graffiti, and apathy. The neighborhood appeared to feel bad about itself. That's what Paul thought, sitting on the stoop of his apartment building. "This," he said, gesturing with a sweep of his arm, "is a place that has low self-esteem."

"I know it," his buddy Roger agreed. "But I guess you can't make a building feel good about itself. Look at all these apartments, just rotting away, disintegrating under the car exhaust."

"Man, you are depressing me no end," said Paul. "We can't let this happen. Not to us. This is where we live. You know that whole thing, a man's home is his castle? We have to do something for our castle."

"Oh man, it's too much, Paul. Where are you going to start?"

"Like my wife says, every good thing starts with a plate of cookies. Follow me." The two men stood up and collared everyone else on their floor that they could find, and they all sat down to talk over a plate of chocolate chip cookies in Paul's kitchen. That was how the Gardens Apartment Complex Society started, and how their building raised its self-esteem.

⊙ Have a reception in the lobby or a barbecue in the backyard. Get everyone's name, apartment number, phone number, and e-mail address. Create a sign-up sheet asking the residents to state their level of willingness to participate and their areas of interest. Show how working together will benefit all of you by reminding residents how a unified front gets things done because it can put more pressure on management to do repairs and provide adequate safety than could one renter or tenant.

- Have monthly meetings to keep track of new problems, brainstorm solutions, and report on the results of prior problem-solving efforts. This is also a chance to socialize with your neighbors and to share what is going on in your lives.

- Identify the main areas that keep an apartment building functioning well, both outside and in. Outside, clean up around the property: pick up trash and cigarette butts, have adequate garbage cans, landscape the property with bushes that do not obstruct doors or windows, and make sure there are bright lights outside the front door and at outdoor parking areas. Think about motion-detecting lights, or those that are sensitive to decreasing light and go on at twilight. Cleanliness inside the building encourages respect for the property. Talk with the manager about cleaning regularly and even about fresh paint, and improved lighting—bright, energy-saving lights help create a cheery atmosphere, prevent accidents due to dimness, and improve safety. Show the manager how these improvements will benefit both the landlord and the residents by reducing accidents—and insurance premiums.

- Identify those neighbors who might be home during the day and can be an emergency contact for children or seniors.

- Volunteers can walk through the building looking for broken locks, burnt-out bulbs, and so on.

- Ask the local police to assess the security needs of your complex. Organizing security for your own building can inspire the residents of surrounding buildings. Encourage people in other apartment buildings and homeowners in your neighborhood to form a watch group with your building (see page 114).

- Keep neighbors apprised of building goings-on by phone, e-mail, or a note under the door. Think about doing a building newsletter or monthly memo. This keeps residents informed on a regular basis of any mutual concerns, and it is also a chance for you to toot your own horn about the improvements your group has made.

⊙ Hope increases and neighbors are motivated to keep things functioning smoothly when residents are house-proud and feel involved and empowered to make a difference.

ELDER CARE CO-OPS

"My husband," Shirley confided to her therapist, "is a dead man talking. He doesn't know who he is, who I am, what year it is, what country we're in. But if I walk out of the room for even a minute, he starts calling, 'Hello . . . hello . . . hello,' continuously until I go back in. It's driving me nuts."

She was describing what many caregivers to Alzheimer's patients feel—a combined sense of loss and of being trapped. They become prisoners in their homes because a disabled spouse needs constant monitoring and supervision. "I swear it was easier with three children," she went on. "At least I could get a baby-sitter once in a while. I'd give anything to have a night out."

And that's when the lightbulb went on. "You know," she said, "we used to have a baby-sitting co-op years ago—a group of parents who would watch each other's kids. Everybody listed the nights and hours they were available for child care, and we had a rotating coordinator for the whole thing. The coordinator would call you up to see if you could baby-sit John and Jill on a certain night. If you said yes, their parents would drop them off. I wonder . . ."

Two months later, Shirley advertised a little group called Elder Care Friends, which would include both caregivers and senior volunteers who wanted to help. They met at the Sunset Senior Center while the Alzheimer's patients were in a morning activity group. Initially, there were four volunteers and eight caregivers. The first meeting began with a single question: who wanted some time off from caregiving responsibilities? Eight hands went up.

Elder Care Friends has similarities in its structure to the old baby-sitting co-op. There's a rotating coordinator. And some of the "elder-sitting" involves caregivers bringing their spouses to each other's homes. Volunteers also provide elder sitting; their payoff is coming to socials hosted by Elder Care Friends at the senior center.

The result of this effort? A woman who'd been angry and overwhelmed was now going out to movies and the symphony. Plus, she'd made some friends who shared a very personal understanding of the challenges of caregiving.

If you'd like to start an elder care group, here are some steps to begin:

- Identify a local senior center that has a program for Alzheimer's patients. Advertise via newsletter or flyer for both caregivers and volunteer seniors.

- Give the co-op a name and appoint yourself its first coordinator. Set a time to meet—a good choice is while Alzheimer's patients are in a program at the center.

- Ask each person to describe special caregiving challenges, particularly dangerous or problematic behaviors of his or her loved one. Take notes. This will give you a chance to identify a situation that might frighten or overwhelm other members. You can either tailor—make plans for these patients—or decide that they not be included in the co-op.

- Make a list of everyone's available hours—both caregivers and volunteers.

- Set a time for a (once-monthly at minimum) social gathering for your group. This can function as both a support meeting for caregivers and as a reward for volunteer participants.

- Make sure there are written elder-sitter instructions for each Alzheimer's patient, with emergency numbers and "what to do if . . ." details. These instructions should be photocopied and given to everybody.

- Some elder care groups are structured so that each caregiver has a "bank account" of hours worked that he or she can cash in for some elder-sitting. The coordinator keeps records of all these accounts.

STOPPING TEEN VIOLENCE

When the kid in Barry's neighborhood would come toward him on the sidewalk, Barry would pretend to be very interested in something on the other side of the street and would cross the street without making eye contact. He couldn't stand the sight of the kid, who was probably about sixteen or seventeen, with a shaved head, a dog collar with spikes around his neck, and several piercings in each ear and one in his nose.

"He just looked like a freak," says Barry. "I could tell he was trouble. So I did what everyone on my street did—got out of his way, avoided him. I pretty much avoided everyone in the twelve to twenty-four age group, to be totally honest with you. My daughter's in college, but she was never like that, like these kids. Freaks of nature is what I called them. If you had asked me six months ago if I thought of a kid like that as part of my community, I would have laughed at you. Things have changed. I've changed."

One morning a neighbor casually mentioned that a teenager had beaten up someone two days earlier and that the victim had ended up in St. Mary's Hospital with broken ribs and a fractured hand. Barry immediately thought that kid was involved, and he was right. But the kid was the victim, not the assailant. The perpetrator was actually a twenty-five-year-old—part of Barry's "safe" age group—who didn't like the look of the teenager.

"He thought the kid was a freak," Barry says, with a cough to hide his emotion. "So he beat him up. It was one of those moments for me when the world just looked different, and I realized that I wanted to do something about this. I wanted it stopped in some way, and it had to start with me. First, I found out where that kid lived and I went and apologized to him for being stupid and closed minded. And he told me so much about himself, about what kids his age go through, the bullying and the pressure and the dangers." Barry now uses his background in business to train teens in running a small business, giving them an experience with handling money, providing a service, and dealing with customers.

The famous psychoanalyst Erik Erikson felt that society needs to provide healthy ways for teens to experiment with different roles, resisting the impulse to create a set-in-concrete label for adolescents who are struggling and who may be taking some wrong turns. There are many stereotypes about teenagers. Many people believe that teens are responsible for a lot of the violence in this country, but the vast majority of serious crime is committed by adults, some of it against teenagers. If you are ready to stop seeing adults and teens in an "us versus them" light, here are some things that can help you get started:

- Encourage your business to donate to after school programs for teens. If there aren't such programs, contact local civic leaders, social service agencies, and law enforcement agencies for help in creating some.

- Solicit help from parents, teachers, counselors, and social workers, as well as others in the community who can offer time and energy to working with teens. Establish a goal of bridging the gap between adults and teenagers by creating dialogue and support. Offer help, not hostility. Meet regularly.

- A group of motivated people could create a neighborhood center that would be more than a place to hang out. Ask about using space in a school after hours when many kids would otherwise be on their own. The center could offer workshops on conflict resolution, anger management skills, bullying prevention, education on child abuse, and alcohol and drug abuse. Peer counseling, whereby teens could help each other under the supervision of a teacher or therapist, is another valuable project. When positive opportunities and support increase for teenagers, their risk of substance abuse, school delinquency and dropping out, and violence decreases. Each person contributes what they can; no one shoulders the burden alone. When Hillary Clinton said it takes a village to raise a child, she was right.

EARTHQUAKE PREPAREDNESS COMMITTEE

The idea for the earthquake preparedness group had its birth when Jane and Polly met, literally, in the middle of the street minutes after the Northridge quake.

Jane and Polly called neighbors together for the first meeting of the earthquake preparedness committee EPC two months later, while interest was still high. Jane had already accumulated earthquake awareness pamphlets and arranged for a group discount for purchasing earthquake preparedness items from a local hardware store. Coffee and tea, accompanied by a "fallen down" chocolate cake, were served. The bulk of the meeting consisted of the formation of various subcommittees, each focusing on a different task. Polly had prepared a list of the tasks to be accomplished. Each subcommittee chairperson was responsible for recruiting additional members. It was suggested that meetings be held on a rotating basis, to involve as many people as possible.

When all the tasks had been assigned to a chairperson, the group decided to meet again in a month to assess its progress. And at the next meeting all chairpersons reported some progress. An additional benefit of rotating meeting places was also discovered: the committee could tour each house and assess earthquake risks; they could also learn to feel comfortable in each other's homes.

In less than six months, all the subcommittees had finished their tasks. Jane supervised the production of the final report, an eight-page document that was a primer on neighborhood earthquake preparedness. This was distributed to all homeowners on the block. A side benefit of the project was that new friendships were created, and at least one romance blossomed.

Here is a list of essential tasks for your earthquake preparedness group:

⊚ Prepare a list of items in a home earthquake kit, and assemble a sample kit. For example: a special tool used to turn off the gas and water supplies at their outside sources; a flashlight; a battery operated radio; lots of spare batteries; and plenty of fresh drinking water.

- Prepare a list of potential hazards in the home, and of what can be done to minimize the danger. For example: fastening bookshelves and china cabinets to the wall; installing latches on cupboards; and securing water heaters with plumbing tape.

- Form a utility safety group. The main task of this group is to visit each home on the block and locate the shutoff valves for both gas and water.

- Prepare a list of community resources—who on the block has useful tools to share in an emergency? For example: a chain saw, a large crowbar, or a backyard hot tub that could provide an emergency water supply.

- Prepare a schematic of every house on the block and a list of all family members (including pets) and telephone numbers for each household. Prepare a schematic or map of the whole block, too, indicating gas and water shutoffs for each building.

- Form a child care group. The task is to identify all the homes with children and list them by name and age. In the event of an earthquake, this group would check on all the children and assemble them in a safe backyard.

- Prepare a list of reliable contractors who do earthquake upgrades (like sheer walls in the basement).

- Form a first aid group. This group's task is to assemble a community cache of emergency first aid supplies—including antibiotics, painkillers, bandages and splints, and crutches—which should be stored in an outdoor shed or other location that will probably be accessible after an earthquake. After the earthquake, this group would erect a first aid tent in a safe backyard.

HELPING THE HOMELESS

Abby never thought much about what it meant to be homeless. The homeless were a group, a category that had nothing to do with her, even though she considers herself to be a kind person who is polite to others and gives to charity. "I came in for a real shock that shook up my preconceived notions but good," she says. On her way to the department store to buy a Halloween costume for her four-year-old daughter, Abby passed a woman sitting on the sidewalk on a blanket with a coffee tin in front of her. The woman looked somehow familiar. Stopping abruptly in front of the doorway to Macy's, Abby realized who the woman was. Pauline had lived on the same floor of the same dorm as Abby in college.

"Pauline was a wonderful girl, a theater major with a quirky sense of humor. She was part of a group of us who hung out at 2 P.M. every day to watch *General Hospital*. To tell you the truth, my first reaction was to pretend that I hadn't recognized her, to just forget about it. And then I went back outside and introduced myself. Of course she remembered me, and was clearly embarrassed by her situation. I was brought up not to make people uncomfortable and had this urge to move on after saying hi. But something made me invite her to have tea with me right then."

Abby learned that Pauline had a child as well, and had gone through a divorce from a man who then left town and paid no child support. The emotional and financial pressure of caring for her son alone led to her being let go at work. Within three months, they ended up in a family shelter.

This information mobilized Abby to take action. Believing that just writing a check was too unsatisfying, she contacted her daughter's school and her church about an ongoing drive to assist people without homes. A core group of five began to meet and collect needed food, clothing, and personal items, as well as information on local social services to be disseminated every Saturday morning at the church. "I've learned that there are many reasons for homelessness and that our society has these stereotypes about the homeless that don't apply," Abby says. "Your friends or family could be only a few paychecks away from living on the streets, and that is the hard truth I've discovered from this. Taking action in this way makes me feel connected to the people I do the drive with, as well as to the people we are trying to help. Pauline meets with us now and is getting back on her feet."

In San Francisco alone, there are over 10,000 people who are homeless on any given day. If you want to assist the homeless, here are some tips for starting a group:

- Treat everyone respectfully. None of us would seem attractive without the possibility of regular showers and clean clothes, and this does not alter who we are as people. Acceptance of the person goes a long way toward feeding self-respect and self-esteem.

- On a computer, create cards that provide information on social services, shelters, showers, health care, and who serves hot meals.

- All group members should go through their closets. Anything you haven't worn in a year could be donated. Cold weather clothes like sweaters and coats are especially needed.

- Families are homeless, too. Collect baby items like diapers, baby powder, and infants' and children's clothes, as well as toys for all ages. Remember that holidays can be a particularly hard time for homeless kids—maybe your group can do a toy drive for Christmas.

- Collect personal care items like bar soap and waterless soap, shavers and deodorant, hair brushes and tampons.

- For your donation drives, meet regularly to decide who does what. Have a regular time and day to give out the items, and get the word out to those agencies who provide services to the homeless.

RESURRECTION OF A SMALL TOWN

Rebecca was dying a slow death. Not literally, of course, but it sure felt like it living in the cultural desolation of Copperton (population 5,027). And her children were suffering as well. The only culture they were exposed to was the mold in the leftover jar of peaches in the back of the refrigerator.

Once Copperton had been a booming mining town. The mines had been laced with rich blue-green veins, and copper prices were high. In those days, the town had a grand movie theater, the Blue Angel, a small scale version of the RKO Coliseum in New York. When the theater closed in the 1980s, it sounded the death knell for the downtown area.

Rebecca was commiserating with her friend Hildy over lunch one day. That's when Hildy said, "You know, a movie theater is the heart and soul of a small town." If the cultural life of the town was to be resurrected, the friends agreed, it would have to start with the movie theater. Then and there, Rebecca hatched an idea to restore the theater to its former glory and transform it into a multipurpose venue.

Her first step was to find the old owner and see if the theater was for sale. It was! And for a reasonable amount. Next, Rebecca approached the downtown merchants and restaurant owners who would benefit most from increased foot traffic in the area. The downtown merchants association agreed to donate $50,000 if matching funds could be generated from the community.

To kick off the community fund-raising campaign, Rebecca arranged to have the block on which the theater was located closed to traffic from noon to five on a balmy Saturday in late September. Local restaurateurs provided free food and beverages on trestle tables. A clown was hired to make little balloon animals. Flyers were distributed inviting everyone in town to attend, bringing cookies to share. As a final touch, a life-sized picture of Marlene Dietrich, top hat and all, was mounted on a cardboard stand and stationed in front of the theater. A photographer with a Polaroid camera was on hand to take souvenir photos of anyone wanting to pose in front of the theater.

At the height of attendance, Rebecca gathered the crowd in front of the theater and delivered her pitch. It was an impassioned plea for the cultural life of the town and the needs of the children. She talked about her plan to use the theater as a place not only for showing classic movies, but for other events as well. Some of the immediate possibilities included a lecture series and a venue for the high school drama club to perform. Part of the space could be utilized as a museum commemorating the town's history.

Sign-up cards were circulated in the crowd requesting donations and volunteer labor to help restore the theater. Since the lobby needed to be retiled anyway, people were invited to buy tiles and sign them for $10 apiece. More affluent patrons could sponsor a new theater seat: a $150 donation bought a brass plaque with the donor's name attached to the back of the seat.

The downtown event was a big success. Donations from all sources easily met the requirements of the matching fund. It took another year and a half, however, to complete the project. The rest of the money needed trickled in slowly; it included a grant, the proposal for which was written by the relative of a board member of a major corporation. Dozens of volunteers from the area worked to restore the theater's interior, donating everything from clean-up labor to wiring and plumbing skills.

The final result was a glorious building divided into a 250-seat venue for main attractions and a smaller, 75-seat venue for classic movies. A separate entrance in the rear led to a free museum with rotating exhibits from all over the county.

If you're thinking about a similar project:

- Seek major backing from local associations that may benefit financially.

- Attract a large crowd for the beginning of the fund-raising campaign. Free food and entertainment are good draws.

- Allow lots of ways to get people involved aside from giving money. Bringing cookies, volunteering an hour of pushing a broom, and other such tasks gives lots of people a sense of pride in and ownership of the project.

- Tap hidden local resources. Community members may have family or business contacts in high places, so don't be shy about asking anyone and everyone to think creatively about fund-raising.

KEEPING IN TOUCH
WITH YOUR FRIENDS

She called it *Nutcase News*. That was the title over a photocopied letter Sharon sent to her friends in June 1987. She was telling the story of a panic attack that had landed her in the emergency room two weeks earlier.

"I have seen the face of self-induced terror," *Nutcase News* began, "and it looks suspiciously like my own." The style was wry and self-effacing, with a good dollop of cliff hanger–type storytelling. Everybody loved it. Sharon suddenly heard from more of her friends than she had in any of the ten years since graduating college. She was getting to catch up on a lot of their stories as well as sharing her own.

One evening Sharon got a call from Adolpho, an unemployed hang gliding instructor. He'd always been a class clown, and as usual he immediately cracked her up. "Want to know how I got unemployed? I volunteered to teach hang gliding to my boss's girlfriend—so she could surprise him. But the girl was a little light on steering skills; she ended up landing in the middle of the Santa Monica Freeway . . . put that in the *Nutcase News*," he said.

And that's exactly what Sharon did. Adolpho's offhand remark gave her an idea that's still going fourteen years later: a newsletter to keep all of her friends in touch. Not just with Sharon's news, but with stories about each of them. Mostly funny. Or celebratory. But occasionally sad and cautionary.

Here's how the *Nutcase News* works. Every four months the news gets published. In the preceding weeks, friends from all over the country start calling Sharon with stories and funny tidbits for the next edition. Tara, for instance, is a world traveler who always has two packed suitcases—one with ski clothes and one with beach clothes. She called to report that she took a Caribbean cruise with the wrong suitcase.

Sometimes the news has a more serious tone, like when Veronica called to report that she had flunked out of law school (Sharon actually thought this was good news), or when Lucy had a miscarriage. If Sharon hasn't heard from a friend for a few issues, she calls to collect a *Nutcase News* "nugget"—some story, no matter how trivial, that will keep them in touch.

A few years ago, Sharon's friends organized a Nutcase reunion. People came from all over the country to reconnect—and to toast Sharon. The toast Sharon remembers best was from Ron, her lab partner in sophomore chemistry. "There have been times," he said, "when the old days seem a distant memory, too long ago to mean anything now. But then the *Nutcase News* arrives, and you all become vividly real again. I feel the strength of our friendships across the miles and years. Thank you, Sharon, for holding us all together."

If you'd like to start your own newsletter for far-flung friends, here are some suggestions to get you started:

- Create a mailing list of as many friends as you can. Put the names and addresses on a computer database so you can print them out on envelopes or mailing labels.

- It's okay if your friends don't all know each other. They'll get acquainted through your newsletter. Write news items so they start with identifying information about your friend, or perhaps a sentence about where you met, for the benefit of readers who don't know them.

- In the beginning, you'll have to call everyone for stories to get it going. After a while, friends will start contacting you with tidbits for the newsletter. Don't worry if you're doing 70 percent of the calling. The main benefit of starting a newsletter is that it gives you an excuse to keep in touch.

- When a friend mentions something that could be an item for your newsletter, get lots of details so you can turn it into a rich, interesting story. Write your stories with lightness and humor, but be careful not to sound like you're making fun of people. If a story is sad, tell it simply, without pathos. Most people get very uncomfortable if you make a big deal about their troubles.

- Set a regular publication schedule of not more than three or four times a year. Then stick to it. More friends will call if the newsletter comes out consistently.

STAY-AT-HOME MOMS

"You know there's this commercial on TV these days . . . I don't know if you've seen it. This woman spends all day talking baby talk to her toddler and then her husband comes home and she's saying things like, 'Did you have a good day at worky jerky?' and he looks at her like she's from another planet. So he takes her to a play and she becomes an adult again. If only it were that simple wimple." At this last statement, which Connie says with a straight face, ten women break into peals of laughter born of complete understanding.

"I think what scared me," Dale says, "is that it's okay to share the wonderful parts with some people, but they get so uncomfortable when I say it's also really lonely being at home all day with my daughter. I once said that I thought my brain had disintegrated, that my IQ had dropped by ten points, and my sister, who doesn't have kids, patted my knee and said 'There, there. It'll be better when she goes to school.' Can you believe that?" She passes a tray of pasta salad across to another women amid murmurs of empathy.

"That's why these meetings are so important to me," says Jennifer, a woman with three children. Her oldest child, a sixteen-year-old, is baby-sitting a crowd of little ones in the next room. "You guys really get it and you also see me for more than what I am as a mom. I really like that we added the personal creativity part to the meeting. I have a poem I wrote last week; I don't know if it's any good, but I realized I was very excited to bring it today to read."

⦿ Finding other mothers who want to be a part of a community will not be difficult. As a mom, you will meet other mothers everywhere you take your child—the park, the pediatrician's office, the nursery school. Post a notice about your group in these places. Since more and more dads are choosing to be at home with their kids, or are single parents, they might want to think about starting their own group.

⦿ It is a given that stay-at-home moms are constantly on the move and often exhausted. That's why the name of the game here has to be tolerance and sharing.

Everyone has to pitch in with everything and really share the responsibility for the gathering. Each mom takes turns hosting a get-together. It should be understood that housecleaning for such an event should be "good enough," not perfect.

- Everyone brings a little something to eat for a potluck. No elaborate dishes unless the mom in question finds relaxation in cooking. The point is to join in sharing something healthy and easy to put together: fruit plates, vegetable assortments and salsa, and sandwiches are all good choices.

- In rotation, each person agrees to find someone to give a short talk once a month on a topic of interest to parents. Speakers can be a child's teacher, a pediatrician, or a therapist talking about the stress of balancing kids and marriage. The speaker can donate the time for a good purpose, getting to know mothers in the neighborhood by staying to chat afterward. Other ideas for topics include tips on how to keep good boundaries, how to keep kids busy during vacations, nutrition to help replenish exhausted parents, and personal care tips.

- Child care should be provided by enterprising teens from families in the group or from the neighborhood. If everyone pitches in, the teen can experience responsibility and make a little money as well. The designated sitter can show videos, play games, and have a story hour.

- On a rotating basis, each person should be encouraged to share something from her life that doesn't involve her kids. This lets each person know she has worth in addition to being a mother. Reading poems, essays, or journal entries, or playing an instrument, helps mothers keep in touch with the rest of themselves.

- At the end of the meeting, before reclaiming their children, all moms help with the cleanup. This should be a given. Too often, the host of a get-together says, "Never mind, I'll do it." It is important that everyone work together and share the chores as well as the satisfaction and joys of being with each other.

SALON

Boring, boring, boring. Elizabeth was used to the intellectual excitement of a big city. She had been happily bicoastal for most of her life, but now sadly found herself in America's heartland. When her husband, Doug, had gotten a teaching job at a college in a small town, she thought it could be fun. And it was at first: buying a house with a big living room and fireplace, and furnishing it with regional antiques; taking wonderful hikes in the hills.

All too soon, the honeymoon summer was over. Doug started spending his days teaching and his evenings researching a journal article. Elizabeth, a free spirit, began to feel lonely and isolated. She thought about finding a job, but couldn't scare up any enthusiasm for being a clerk in the local minimall. What she really wanted was to be surrounded by creative people—people with new ideas and novel perspectives on life.

Elizabeth decided that the best place to start was by volunteering her time at the arts institute attached to the college where her husband taught philosophy. She had a master's degree in art, and soon she was filling in for teachers who called in sick. The next semester, she was offered a job teaching an art history class.

That's how she met a number of bright, talented students who seemed to need her encouragement. She came to realize that what these students needed was more freedom to develop their ideas outside the narrow confines of academe. She began to invite some of them for Sunday afternoon tea, which became a regular event featuring gourmet finger sandwiches and lively interactions. Elizabeth would often begin an afternoon by suggesting a topic for discussion, such as "the value of empty space in sculpture" or "the Japanese influence on Monet." Additional members of the biweekly teas were added by invitation only.

There was more to these Sundays than just tea and talk. The intellectual sky was the limit. Members were encouraged to bring in their original work for feedback. One student, Una, brought in a performance piece combining music, movement, poetry, and large sculptures.

Elizabeth was reminded of the concept of the salon—a regular gathering of witty creative people. Her college heroines had been Madame de Staël and Alma Werfel Gropius Mahler, who had created salons where the air crackled with wit and intelligent conversation. A salon was not just a place (although her living room was a perfect place for gatherings), but a supportive environment where people could gather to exchange ideas. That's what she and her students were engaged in.

The salon became more than just an opportunity for its members to try out new ideas and get emotional and psychological support for revolutionary work. The support extended to the material plane as well, since Elizabeth had contacts with people in the philanthropic community who could be persuaded to provide the occasional seed grant for promising artistic projects. She even had a shed out back that served as an emergency crash pad for artists down on their luck.

The Sunday teas were eventually supplemented by a monthly Friday night soirée, which featured wine tasting, hors d'oeuvres, and a visiting guest. In the beginning, the guest was a local poet or artist. Over time, news of Elizabeth's salon spread by word of mouth through the college campus network. Authors on book tours angled for an invitation. Artists showing new work in any gallery within a one hundred-mile radius made discreet phone calls asking for the opportunity to put in an appearance. Elizabeth was no longer bored.

Tips for starting a salon:

⊙ Begin by forming an affiliation with an established institution, like a local college or arts organization: volunteer, enroll, or get involved in another way.

⊙ Provide a supportive environment where people feel safe in trying out new, innovative thoughts or projects. The salon should nourish its members both emotionally and physically.

⊙ Develop an air of exclusivity: new members should be able to join by invitation only, and the group's size should be limited. This allows the group to keep the best and brightest.

CONNECTING IN CYBERSPACE

When Julie's husband was transferred from New York to Wisconsin, she lost more than proximity to her family and friends. One of Julie's deepest loves is horses and, apart from missing her father (who is a small-time thoroughbred horse trainer), Julie missed the community she had become part of by knowing people in the horse racing business.

With no track nearby, Julie could watch races on television, but there was no one around who shared her intense love of the thoroughbred. "We suddenly had room to keep two horses, but it felt lonely and isolating without the contact with the trainers and grooms and exercise riders I had known all my life. That first year when we watched the Kentucky Derby in our living room, screaming at the television by ourselves, my husband and I both realized we had to do something different."

Julie got onto the Internet and typed in "horse racing" on various search engines. "I have now been part of a group of friends, some of whom I have never met face to face, for almost four years. Keri, whom I met through the message boards, had an extra ticket to the Belmont Stakes one year, and I had the amazing experience of meeting her and some other people from the boards, and then introducing them to my dad, who met us there. When my horse, Charmer, became really ill, the folks on the boards were incredibly supportive and even helped me find a veterinary specialist. When he got through the night and we knew he was going to make it, I couldn't wait to get on the computer to tell everyone the good news. I read some of their messages to me with tears running down my cheeks. They are awesome people."

The Internet has provided a way to overcome the limits of time, space, and money for many people. As long as you have a computer with access to the Internet—and you don't even have to own your own these days—you are set. Libraries and even some coffee shops are providing access to the Internet for patrons at little or no cost. With just a little effort, anyone can become part of an online community.

⊙ Make a list of your interests and your needs. What do you want to know more about or need help with? If you could have a conversation about something, no matter how esoteric or off the wall, what would that subject be?

- Using a search engine (such as Google or Yahoo!), do a search using key words that indicate what you are looking for (like "windsurfing" or "antique collecting"). You can also help your search by typing "online community" into a search engine and then looking at the results for something that piques your interest.

- Many community-based Web sites offer several ways to participate, such as chat rooms, which are live and have a moderator, and message boards, which are not as immediate, but can reflect conversations and discussions that have occurred over the last hours, days, or even months.

- Try out a number of different chat rooms and message boards. Like any group of people—even one with common interests—each has its own character and flavor. Some message boards have a monitor who makes sure there is no offensive language being used; culprits may be warned and then even banned. Other boards are more permissive, each person being responsible for his or her own behavior.

- Many people feel more comfortable just "lurking," which means reading everyone else's comments and posts, and saying nothing themselves. This is fine if your purpose is to learn or to be entertained. If you want more, however, you will need to take the next step and—say something! If your question doesn't get answered or your opinion doesn't get addressed, don't despair and don't take it personally, just repost it.

- Since no one can see or hear each other, in order to avoid misunderstandings people talking online use "emoticons," such as :-) (smile) and ;-) (smile and wink), and online shorthand such as "IMHO" (in my humble opinion). Hopefully, you can find a place online where you feel connected and supported and where you can "lol" (laugh out loud) with a new group of friends.

BUILD A WEB SITE

Randi Kreger knew what it was like to walk on eggshells. Over the years she'd had to cope with a number of friends who all shared a particular sensitivity to criticism, and who displayed Jekyll-and-Hyde-like reactions to stress. Sometimes they were loving and sweet; at other times the tiniest provocation would send them into eye-popping rages. No amount of caution on Randi's part seemed enough to prevent the explosions.

But anger wasn't the only problem. Small rejections or failures could trigger black depression, threats of suicide, or panic in these people. Their emotions often moved from tame to out of control in the space of a few minutes. And the roller coaster just kept on going—day after day, year after year.

In her quest to understand what was going on, Randi learned about something called borderline personality disorder (BPD). This is a psychiatric diagnosis that describes people who are excruciatingly sensitive to rejection and cope with it by using anger and a defense called *splitting*. When you split, you separate the world into two groups—those who are all good and those who are all bad. You love and depend on those who are good; you punish and attack the bad guys. There's no in between. Folks with BPD will also suddenly decide that someone who was once considered all good is really bad. And they will unpredictably attack and rage at that person.

All the problem behavior that Randi had observed in certain friends suddenly had a label. And Randi learned another important thing: BPD is a common problem, affecting as many as 6 million people in the U.S. Which means that there are millions more who have a family member or friend with BPD. Most of these folks struggle alone, coping as best they can with all the volatility, having no idea what BPD is or how it affects their loved one.

Randi decided to create a source of information and support for people who are in relationship to someone with BPD. In order to reach the largest audience, Randi started a Web site called bpdcentral.com. The Internet, she says, is like a colossal support group "in the biggest church basement in the world."

The Web site contains a lot of helpful information on coping, plus a message board where folks can share their experiences and personal strategies. Therapists offer counsel regarding some of the thorny issues discussed on the message board. The site was an instant success and now boasts thousands of hits a day.

If you'd like to develop an Internet support group, or any Web community, here are some suggested guidelines:

- Identify your site focus. Web communities can form around virtually any shared interest (fandom, collecting, hobbies) or problem. Check what's already about there to make sure you aren't duplicating someone else's effort. If there are similar sites to what you're planning, decide how yours can be different.

- If you have the skill, program your own Web site using HTML or Java Script. Help is available from FrontPage and other site authoring programs. If you don't have the time or knowledge to do this yourself, you can (1) place an ad for a Web publishing programmer on an Internet job line, or (2) have IBM build your Web site for you. Your Web programmer will usually help you find an appropriate server.

- Start small. After developing a home page, you can add special features and new content over time. Building and maintaining a Web site is a lot of work, so pacing is important.

- To attract attention, your Web site will need helpful information about the target issue or problem. Getting content is easy. You can search other Web sites, books, or periodicals for information. Be sure to put everything in *your own words* to avoid charges of plagiarism.

- Always include information about additional resources, plus links to related sites and organizations.

- In addition to helpful information, your Web site may include a message board, a chat room, or both, so people can trade information or give each other support.

Once up and running, you should monitor the message board to delete inappropriate messages, as well as to answer questions.

⊙ It's often helpful to secure the services of a volunteer expert to field difficult questions on the message board.

⊙ Make sure people can find you. You or your programmer should submit your site to the appropriate search engines. Check into the advantages of creating a "Web ring" with other related sites.

⊙ Get linked. Find the e-mail addresses of Web masters on related sites and make a request to exchange links.

⊙ Encourage your message board participants to share experiences, ask informational questions, offer suggestions, or provide emotional support. Don't let them turn the board into a soap box or a place where people get attacked. The key is creating an environment where people feel safe enough to share and be open.

⊙ Many helpful resources for Web publishing have been published; one such is *Foundation Dreamweaver Ultra Dev 4* by Rob Paddock and Spencer Steel (2001).

PEER CONSULTATION

Denny was proud to be a computer nerd in Silicon Valley, but now he was stuck. He needed help—big time. This project (the project from hell) was going to be the end of him, unless he could come up with a new approach. Thinking "outside the box" seemed impossible. He felt multiboxed in, like a box within a box within a box. So he decided that the only reasonable thing to do was to go to the Computer Café around the corner and shoot some darts.

"This damn problem is driving me crazy," he complained between sips of beer while waiting his turn at the dartboard. "What problem is that?" a friendly neighbor asked. "It's pretty esoteric stuff, writing source code for a new interactive software product," Denny replied. "Yeah, that's out of my field," the neighbor conceded. "What you really need to do is to assemble a think tank of specialists in that area of expertise. I'll bet a lot of people around here are in the same boat as you," his neighbor continued. "And probably lots of others all over the world as well."

That's when Denny got the idea of mounting a two-pronged attack on the problem. He would "think globally and act locally": in order to maximize his potential to get help, he would establish two different types of peer consultation group. Both would be run the same way, with a freewheeling, anything-goes style of brainstorming. But one would "actually" meet, in his living room, and the other would meet "virtually," in a private chat room on the Internet.

Denny also realized that he was not good at organizing, so he decided to call his old friend Joan and enlist her help—she worked in the Valley herself. They met for lunch a few days later, and Joan suggested creating an "A" list and a "V" list. The A list began with some people they both knew, either from college or from conventions they had attended. All of them either lived or worked within a twenty-mile radius. They split up the list and made personal phone calls. Those interested in but not available for the actual group formed the nucleus of the V list. Some of the people Denny and Joan contacted suggested others who might be interested.

The next step was to get the word out on the Internet. They put notices in the most obvious places: www.SiliconValley.internet.com and www.SVdaily.com. These generated several interested responses as well. Again, potential community members were placed on the A or V list.

The A list members, seven in all including Denny and Joan, met within a week. Denny fortified the group with an unlimited supply of pizza and soft drinks. The group agreed to 1) be mutually supportive, 2) maintain confidentiality, and 3) meet as needed. Anyone could call a meeting for a brainstorming session, but Denny's problem was first on the agenda.

To accommodate the people on the V list, Denny created a Web site with a link to a private chat room. All potential members were prescreened, assigned unique screen names, and given a password "key" to the chat room. The V group agreed to check in once a week at the appointed time to help any member who felt stuck with a problem. Denny was the first person to be the beneficiary of this group as well.

It worked! Denny was able to use all the consulting help he'd gathered to create a breakthrough in the project from hell. The two groups continue to meet and have actually taken on a social function as well. In fact, Denny and Joan are engaged.

If you want to set up a consultation group, consider the following:

- Technology offers more options than face-to-face meetings. If you need help constructing a Web site, see "Build a Web Site" in this book. Or consider starting a listserv or bulletin board, or joining an existing one (see the chapter "Connecting in Cyberspace.")

- Actual consulting groups need to be nurtured according to their nature: pizza and cola for nerds, paté and wine for execs.

- Begin with people you know and can trust, and add others by these people's recommendation.

- Promote a wide-open atmosphere, where anything goes.

A MEDICAL SUPPORT COMMUNITY

Bonnie Durante kept asking, "Why us? Why can't we live like a normal family?" But Bonnie and her children were anything but normal. Her boy, Jim, had constant difficulties with chest pain, palpitations, fatigue, and digestive problems. The worst thing was his out of control anxiety. It seemed like he had a new phobia every month.

Her daughter, Cheryl, was much the same. "She was terrified twenty-four hours a day." And Bonnie was distressed that symptoms she'd struggled with her whole life had now somehow been passed on to her children.

Despite a constant parade of doctors and tests, even hospitalizations, no one in Bonnie's family ever got better—until 1988. That's when a cardiologist finally suggested the diagnosis of mitral valve prolapse syndrome (MVPS). MVPS, Bonnie learned, can cause weakness, a sped up or irregular heart rate, irritable bowel syndrome, chest pain, and twenty-seven other symptoms. The most devastating symptoms, however, are psychological. More than 80 percent of MVPS folks suffer panic attacks and phobias. Seventy percent are seriously depressed. Most suffer irrational worries that can end up controlling their lives.

Once Bonnie had a name for her nightmare, she got busy finding out what to do about it. She learned that MVPS, while associated with a slight dysfunction of the mitral valve in the heart, is really a problem of the autonomic nervous system. Folks with MVPS get flooded with the hormone epinephrine—better known as adrenaline. That's why they often feel so anxious. Getting better requires a whole regimen that includes exercise, high fluid intake, medication (beta blockers), and avoiding stimulants like caffeine and sugar.

With her family on the road to health, Bonnie turned her attention to helping others. In 1991, she started an MVPS support group in the public library of her hometown. Bonnie built membership in the group through a series of free seminars. She and her family would speak, as would invited experts; the focus was on practical things each person could do to manage MVPS symptoms.

Eventually the support group also began to be publicized through a Web site—www.mitralvalveprolapse.com—which provides medical information, coping advice, and a message board for people to share experiences.

Recently, Bonnie began reaching out to people who are far away from her Itasca, Illinois support group. She started a newsletter called *And the Beat Goes On*, which now has subscribers spread over forty states and eight countries.

Out of a family medical crisis, Bonnie Durante created a support network that connects more than 5,000 people. "I'm a success story," Bonnie says, "and I know they can be, too. I am now living life instead of being a mere presence in it."

You can start your own medical support group by following these steps:

- ◉ Reserve a weekly two-hour block at a library, church, or hospital meeting room.

- ◉ Schedule a medical specialist to speak the first night, and ask him or her to be on your advisory board.

- ◉ Create a single-page flyer with tear-off phone numbers and put it up in the waiting rooms of cooperative physicians. You can also advertise the group with public service announcements on the radio.

- ◉ Each meeting should be structured around either a lecture or a discussion of key symptoms and coping strategies. Then open it up so members can share a wide range of concerns, getting support and advice from the group.

- ◉ Make sure the group has at least a few members who have successfully coped with the illness and can be a source of both knowledge and inspiration.

THE VILLAGE

"I've been observing at Megan's kindergarten class, and I'm not happy about what I see," Helena said one evening to Bob.

"What's the problem now?" Bob replied. "We moved to this area specifically because of the excellent reputation of the school system."

"That's true, we did," Helena continued. "But I don't think that Megan is getting as much attention as she deserves. You know how quiet and well-behaved she is. Well, the teacher is focusing most of his attention on the boys who have behavior problems."

"I've heard that happens pretty much all over, that boys get the lion's share of attention. What can we do about it?"

"Well, I've been thinking that we could probably do a better job of educating her at home, and I've been doing some research into the subject."

"Honey, I know that you graduated from Teacher's College, and would have become a teacher if you hadn't gotten pregnant. But do you really think that this is a good idea?"

"Yes, I think I do. And here's how we're going to do it."

That's how Megan's home schooling began. Helena had done her homework. She knew that home education was legal in all fifty states. So the first thing to do was to fill out an application from the state department of education. Next, she would prepare a curriculum for her daughter. Her background in early childhood education gave her a good basis to work from, but she decided to invest in a prepared curriculum from Pleasant Company Publications.

"Okay, honey, I trust you to do a good job on the education front," Bob said reluctantly, "but won't Megan be missing out on being with other kids?"

"You mean the socialization aspect. Yes, I've thought about that too. And here's my plan. . . ."

Helena had already been in contact with the local librarian, who knew about other home school families. She also asked her parish priest, who supplied additional names of families doing home schooling. By calling these families, she got the names of other parents as well. It was amazing how many other parents were interested in home schooling.

So Helena decided to start a newsletter: a small, monthly flyer sharing resources. Eventually, it became a weekly e-mail bulletin, which Helena (influenced by Hillary Clinton) dubbed *The Village*.

The Village helped Helena organize and publicize Park Days, an opportunity for a group of home schoolers to meet once a week in the local park. The kids played together while the parents got to hang out with other adults. As the kids grew older, Park Days evolved into weekly field trips that ranged from visits to the interactive science museum to backstage passes at the local ballet company.

Both Helena and Bob had always been involved in local projects such as the food bank and habitat restoration. It was only natural that Helena incorporated these activities into her home schooling curriculum as well. Other families from "the Village" were glad to join in, seeing their children's participation as an educational opportunity as well as a chance for socialization.

The events of September 11, 2001 proved a challenge to the home schooling community. While public schools were capitalizing on their resources by offering psychological counseling for traumatized families and assembly programs, the Village organized its own response. A small pocket park was chosen as the site for a community gathering. A large altar was erected, and soon it was overflowing with teddy bears and candles. Home school students read poems they had written. Everyone held hands and offered a silent prayer. They were not alone.

When organizing a home schooling community:

- Contact your local librarian, who is usually knowledgeable about other home schoolers.

- For diversity, check with your church or synagogue to contact religious-based home schooling families.

- Start a newsletter, paper or electronic, to get others interested.

- Arrange to meet one day a week for joint activities such as field trips.

- Rally the families for special events.

JACK'S (MEDITATION) ROOM

"What the hell's he doing in there?" asked one of the new ER techs.

"You mean Jack, sitting cross-legged on the gurney like that?"

"That's the dude. They gonna put his picture in the dictionary next to 'weird.'"

"That's Jack's room."

"What are you talkin' about? That's just an empty space waitin' for the next fool who's gotten himself in a gang fight."

"No, it's a bit of a joke around here. Any time it's slow, like tonight, he'll pull a curtain around one of the unused gurneys and sit there in a Buddha pose. Wherever he does it, we call it Jack's room."

"He's got this 'not here' look. Like he just passed Pluto and he ain't stopping."

"He's meditating. God help us, he's got the whole ER doing it."

With that explanation, the new tech was initiated into a most unusual emergency room practice. Jack had been at Mercy Hospital for less than a month when coworkers started noticing his peculiar routine. Jack told anyone who asked that he was a meditator, and that he used meditation to calm the adrenaline rush set off by each emergency case. The staff noticed that Jack was compassionate in his work, and that trauma never appeared to touch him.

"I couldn't get that relaxed on a beach in the Bahamas," said the ward clerk as she watched Jack do his Buddha thing. "I've seen dead people who are less relaxed."

People were intrigued, and several wondered out loud whether meditation might help them. Jack offered to teach anyone who wanted to learn, and invited all the ER folks to his house for a "cheese and meditation" night. To his amazement, a dozen people showed up, and they ate Limburger, Muenster, and Provolone while Jack described some basic principles of meditation: focusing on an object or sound, emptying the mind, and releasing distracting thoughts. People practiced for five minutes at a time, then shared their experiences and got feedback from Jack.

"Cheese and meditation" was an unqualified success, so Jack sponsored another one for a Saturday morning—this time in the meeting room of a local library. Most of the

ER staff showed up, and at this writing the meditation group has met every Saturday morning for the past six years. They have also received permission to use the hospital chapel for meditation breaks during working hours.

Jack still prefers to meditate sitting cross-legged on a gurney. "He's an odd duck," one of the nurses says. "I need peace and quiet to meditate, but he could do it in Grand Central Station."

If you'd like to start your own meditation group, we suggest that you:

- Read *The Three Minute Meditator* by David Harp. It's chock-full of good, brief meditation practices.

- Locate a free meeting hall: libraries or churches are the best bet. Set a consistent time. A weekend morning is best if you're only going to sit together once a week.

- Advertise at work through word of mouth or e-mail broadcasts. You can also find participants by putting flyers up at local schools, laundries, ice cream shops, supermarket bulletin boards, and the like. Emphasize in your advertisement that meditation is the best method ever discovered to achieve deep relaxation, and that participating in a group reinforces and supports regular meditation practices.

- Encourage novices. Have them come thirty to forty-five minutes before each scheduled group sit to get special training and support.

MARTIAL ARTS FOR WOMEN

When Victoria was accosted one night on her way to her car after work, she had a jolt of realization about herself and the world. "He had his hand on my purse and the other one on my arm. He ripped the purse from my shoulder so hard I thought it was dislocated. I think the only reason he didn't hurt me more was because another man at the top of the street saw what was happening, and yelled at him, and the mugger just ran. That's when it really got through to me. I'm sixty-two, and I decided that unless I wanted to feel at the mercy of everyone in the world I'd better do it differently. My friend Joan encouraged me to try martial arts. I felt really odd about it at first. I mean, I'm a Caucasian woman, I'm not Bruce Lee. That's the only thing I knew about it."

Joan doesn't look like Bruce Lee either. A tall, slender college English professor, Joan has been a practitioner of hapkido, a Korean martial art, for several years and will soon test for her black belt. Regarding her martial arts school, or dojo, she talks about the sense of belonging and the bond that occurs among the students and instructors. "Nothing like throwing people around to develop camaraderie!" she says with a laugh.

"Traditionally martial arts schools were home to their students, and this gets carried over in my school. In the past we've had Fourth of July barbecues, Halloween parties, camping trips, and movie nights. We also have incentives for kids—star patches they can wear on their uniforms if they maintain a good GPA, read a certain number of books, or help out around their homes. Lots of parents enroll with their kids. Our school has always made a place for families and that, too, heightens the sense of community."

"My daughter has just enrolled my twelve-year-old granddaughter," says Victoria. "I get so much from being at the dojo. Even though I'm just starting, I feel respected for my willingness to train and give it my all. Everyone is so helpful, no matter who they are. One of the black belts spent time with me after class, helping me out with a technique I was doing incorrectly. I can't tell you how proud I feel of the women of my family becoming strong, disciplined, and capable of defending ourselves."

⊙ Before starting a martial arts course, see your doctor and get a physical, just as you would before beginning any kind of exercise program. If you have particular physical problems, a medical exam may assist you in deciding which martial art is the one for you. As with any other foray into a healthier lifestyle, quitting smoking and eating a balanced diet will help immensely.

- ◉ Choose a martial arts school that is close to home or work, has a good reputation, and has been around for a while. Visit the school itself, look over the facilities, and ask what the student-to-teacher ratio is. Individual attention is important. Another criterion should be respect: respect should be shown not just to the higher ranks, but should come from the higher ranks to those at a lower level of training as well.

- ◉ Women who are choosing martial arts for self-defense training should think about a mixed gender dojo. A woman is more likely to be attacked by a man, so being able to train with men can be quite important.

- ◉ Another consideration for women trying to form a sense of community within martial arts is the school's attitude toward socializing. Some may seem more serious and businesslike, with no emphasis on friendships between students; others have an atmosphere more conducive to extracurricular events such as watching martial arts films together or giving exhibitions at local festivals.

- ◉ Make your martial arts training a priority and schedule other things around your classes. Everyone leads busy, harried lives, and it is easy for things that started out as important to us to be shuffled to the back burner. Take classes at least two or three times a week to make this commitment, to improve your skills, and to bond with the people at the dojo.

INTENTIONAL COMMUNITY

Adam was working contentedly in the garden, hoeing a patch of sugar beets. He loved the peaceful environment, the relaxed pace, and the good companionship of others. Less than a year before, he had been living a solitary and lonely life. Then he found Paradise on Earth. Idly, he reflected on what he'd heard of his new community's beginnings from Evelyn, a founding member.

"First of all," Evelyn had said, "Paradise was not the original name of this place. Many of us thought that Paradox would be a more appropriate description of rural living in an urban environment." The idea for this community grew out of a continuing discussion led by a pair of friends in Cambridge, Massachusetts in the seventies. Chris and Robin had known each other since college, and whenever they met with a certain group of old friends, their shared dream of living in an urban community in harmony with nature would inevitably resurface.

Chris had visited various communes during trips to California, and Robin was tired of working in a bureaucratic environment. One night in Cambridge, they finally decided to make the dream a reality. They pooled their money for first and last month's rent, and Chris went to California to find a large house with a big backyard for a garden, no more than forty-five minutes from "civilization." Chris easily found a place south of San Francisco that filled the bill. Robin and some of their other friends from the East Coast all moved into the new house within a couple of months.

At first there were just a few rules: 1) share the rent; 2) recycle; 3) work in the organic garden. For the first couple of years the house functioned as a shared living environment. It was a place where residents who had generally compatible world views paid a fair share of the rent. People would come and go, staying only for as long as it suited their personal needs. Over time, a core group became the constant factor in the house. Chris, Robin, Sandy, and Evelyn, all part of the original settler group, got together one Saturday night and decided it was time to move the community to the next level. Robin had spoken with the landlord and discovered that the house was available for sale. Sandy had some money and was willing to invest it in the future of the group.

These four called a house meeting and invited all the other residents to be part of the new intentional community. The primary "intent" was to be this: "a commitment to pursuing a purposeful, ecologically sound lifestyle, characterized by awareness of self and environment." The group's goal was an egalitarian community based on the premise that everyone was worthy of respect and consideration. The community would be a non-profit (501[c][3]) corporation dedicated to teaching its members ecological principles. In addition to the corporate by-laws, the group agreed they would decide on a list of guidelines for living harmoniously together.

It ended up being quite a list, and took a month of meetings to codify and ratify to everyone's satisfaction. Everything was covered, from dealing with money (each member would make a yearly tithe) to bathroom behavior (leave the toilet with its seat down). Eventually, a third of the group, the more casual residents, chose to drop out. "That's how it all started," Evelyn concluded. "And from then on the Paradise community, like Topsy, just grew. . . ."

If you want to start an intentional community, here are some things to consider:

- Intentional communities take time to build. Expect setbacks. The growth of an intentional community does not follow a linear path.

- It is essential that all members of the community commit to a common set of values (philosophical, ecological, political, and so forth). A written statement of intent will help clarify these values. Rules, or guidelines for living harmoniously, should also be mutually agreed and written down.

- A community of this kind needs both shared, public space and private space for each of its members.

- Involvement in common projects helps the community to solidify; such involvement (cooking, gardening) should be part of membership.

- Consider incorporating the community as a nonprofit, both for tax purposes and to enable you to apply for grants. Nolo Press publishes guidelines and forms to help you do this.

THE ZIPPER CLUB

In 1974, in a hospital outside Philadelphia, Sidney Freedman was recovering from a valve and bypass surgery. This event would have zero historical significance except for one thing. While Sid was still in the hospital, his doctor asked him to visit another patient who was facing the same surgery. This patient was very frightened, the doctor explained, and it might help if he got support from someone who already made it through.

They wheeled Sid down for his visit. When it was over and he was back in his room, Sid had one of those blistering moments of truth. He saw clearly that no matter how good the doctor, there are things no doctor can give. People facing a surgery need the support and empathy of someone who knows what it's like from the inside. At that moment, in the surgical wing of Deborah Heart and Lung Center, the Zipper Club was born.

The very first Zipper Club meeting was held in Sid's home, and was attended by a rabbi, a cardiologist, and maybe a dozen heart patients and their spouses. This nucleus of volunteers began making home and hospital visits to patients referred by local doctors—all people who were facing open-heart surgery. As the Zipper Club has evolved, it has focused mostly on helping pre-op patients get ready by giving them detailed information about what to expect and what the recovery process feels like. Most visits include a showing of the classic, zipperlike scar on the chest of the volunteer. The message: "Here's what it looks like when you've healed, when it's all over. I made it; you'll make it, too."

These days, the Zipper Club serves a large chunk of Pennsylvania and New Jersey. All volunteers complete a special training program and attend monthly meetings where they learn about stress reduction, exercise, healthy nutrition, and other prevention practices. Though Sid eventually retired and went to Florida, land of the palmetto bug, the club continues to prosper. Thousands of open-heart surgery patients have been helped, including Harry. "The Zipper Club," Harry declared, "was an inspiration. I began to believe, for the first time, that I could be well again."

You can start your own medical support volunteer club by taking the following steps:

- Identify patients who have successfully coped with or recovered from a specific medical problem or procedure. Advertise via flyers in doctors' waiting rooms, hospital treatment centers, even drugstores.

- At the first gathering—these often happen in hospital meeting rooms—emphasize that the purpose of the club is service to others, and that the main activity is providing in-person or telephone support for those who are facing a medical crisis. Then have a medical professional give some nuts and bolts training on how to provide that support.

- Offer club members regular opportunities to meet so they can learn more about health building and coping strategies relevant to their illness. These meetings should also offer opportunities to socialize, so make sure you have beverages, snacks, and time for lots of lively discussion. Encourage members to share experiences from their meetings with patients. Funny, poignant, even disappointing—as long as they don't mention names, these stories can be enlightening and meaningful.

FOOD CO-OP

In the musical *Kismet* there is a song that goes, in part, "Why be content with an olive, when you could have a tree . . . ?" Joe was content, at first, with the success of the neighborhood food buying group (see the first chapter in this book for a description). However, he soon started thinking about expanding on the idea. Why not have a whole store dedicated to providing the best fresh and organically grown foods, with member participation?

This idea would probably have stayed in the fantasy stage, but something fortuitous happened. Joe's maiden aunt in Milwaukee died and left him a small inheritance. This allowed him to quit his job (which he hated anyway) and focus on this new project. The first step was an Internet search that turned up the "BriarPatch Community Market," an actual working model of what he had envisioned. The site clearly enunciated the basic principles of the cooperative movement: 1) voluntary and open membership; 2) democratic member control; 3) member economic participation; and 4) concern for community. This was exactly what Joe had in mind.

A little additional searching unearthed a Web site called the "Co-op Primer." There he found a template, adapted from the book *How to Organize a Cooperative* (published by the National Cooperative Business Association), which listed the sequence of steps necessary for the formation of a cooperative venture.

The first step was to assemble a core group. Joe and Maxine (they had met on a food buying run) began by canvassing their friends and acquaintances. Then, they put up flyers in homeopathic vitamin stores, the local branch office of the Sierra Club, massage and yoga centers, and the graduate business department of the local university. What they were looking for was an eclectic mix of people who cared about their bodies and the environment, and had some interest in or experience with business operations. Within six weeks their efforts had paid off, and they were ready to meet.

Everyone in the core group agreed that forming a co-op market was a good idea, so Joe went ahead and designated all present as members of the steering committee. The group's next step would be to conduct a survey of the community to determine whether there was a perceived need for a food co-op, which would help them decide whether such a venture was feasible. Joe presented the group with a sample survey he had created on his computer. The survey outlined the concept of the proposed food co-op, and asked the person filling it out to rate certain aspects of the idea on a scale from 0 to 10, and respond to several yes or no questions:

1. How satisfied are you with the quality of the food you are currently buying? (0 = completely unsatisfied; 10 = completely satisfied)

2. Do you think that there is a need for a co-op food store that would provide you with fresh, organically grown food? (0 = no need at all; 10 = very strong need)

3. How often would you shop at a co-op store if it were available? (0 = never; 10 = as often as possible)

4. Would you be willing to participate in a co-op store to the extent of putting in two hours a week of hands-on work? (yes/no)

5. Would you be willing to buy a membership in a co-op store and become a shareholder? (yes/no)

6. (If interested) name and telephone number: _____

7. Other comments _____

After some discussion, about, for one thing, the price of a membership share ($50 per family), the group agreed to distribute 500 copies of the survey. It was also decided that it would be best if the questionnaires were handled individually and in person. Each member of the core group agreed to hand-distribute fifty copies of the survey. Other than to friends and family, questionnaires would be distributed at members' workplaces, at PTA meetings, and at a table outside the local supermarket.

Three weeks later, the tallies were in, and it seemed that there was indeed a reasonable amount of grassroots support for the co-op market concept. The core group decided that a general meeting should be held at the local public library, where the results of the survey could be presented. Attendance was good, and included many people who had filled out the questionnaire. Attendees were asked to fill out pledge cards indicating their willingness to join the co-op. Interested people were given additional pledge cards to pass on to friends and family members. This proved to be the beginning of a successful membership drive, which also included ads in the local paper and a benefit concert with local talent.

The core group, emboldened by the success of the general meeting, decided to hire a consultant to conduct a market and financial (cost/supply) analysis and to develop a business plan. These are important elements in starting a successful business, and are best undertaken by professionals. Fortunately, there was a local organization that specialized in helping nonprofits get started. They even had a grant to underwrite such projects, so the cost was minimal.

With the help of the consultant and a book from Nolo Press (*How to Form a Nonprofit Corporation* by Anthony Mancuso), the core group got to work. They elected a board of directors, adopted bylaws, and drew up the necessary legal papers to incorporate as a nonprofit (501[c][3]) organization. The final steps of the process included: 1) acquiring capital (this was accomplished through donations from local philanthropists and taking out low interest loans); 2) acquiring a facility (in this a case, the gymnasium of a closed-down school); and 3) hiring a manager and starting up operations.

As a sidelight, Joe and Maxine got married during the course of this project. And their son, Cooper, was born within days of the opening of the new store.

Here is a typical sequence of events for forming a cooperative:

- Identify a core group of interested people and have a meeting to discuss what needs a cooperative could fill.

- Create a steering committee from those most interested.

- Conduct a survey to determine the feasibility of the project.

- Hold a general meeting to discuss the results of the survey and to begin to gather members.

- Hire professional consultants to conduct a financial and market analysis and to create a business plan.

- Draw up the necessary legal documents and incorporate as a nonprofit.

- Call a meeting of all potential charter members to adopt bylaws and elect a board of directors.

- Increase your economic base by conducting a membership drive.

- Acquire capital, including low interest loans as necessary.

- Acquire facilities, hire a manager, and start up operations.

TENNIS, ANYONE?

Men aren't usually much for gab. The typical conversation of guys stuck talking at a party goes like this:

"How's it goin'?"

"Good. Really good." Shuffling, checking the buttons on his shirt.

"How's everything at the office?"

"Same old shit. You know: they keep piling it on, and we keep trying to dig out from under."

"Sally okay?"

"The usual, but she's basically good. You know. Slidin' by any way she can." More button checking.

Uncomfortable laughter. Silence.

"You know, just slidin' down the razor blade of life."

Courtesy laugh. "So how 'bout those Bears?"

Most men *hate* to talk about how they're doing and what they're feeling. It cuts too close to the bone. What works for guys is talking about a task, an event, a shared experience. When men build a community, it pretty much has to be around something they *do* together, an activity that stirs and engages them.

Hence, sports.

Matt plays doubles with a group of men who meet every Saturday morning at eight. Four to six guys usually show up. The man who organized everything has pulled together a diverse ensemble that includes a computer programmer, an architect, two publishers, and his college roommate from twenty-five years ago.

After everyone warms up, the game begins. Here's a sample of the conversation:

"Killer passing shot!"

"Nice volley."

"You put some smoke on that."

"Oh, God! To miss something that fat, that easy. A ball right down Main Street."

"Good game, gentlemen."

It's when the game is over that conversation finally has a chance. Everyone's pumped full of endorphins. Everyone feels that primitive muscle joy they remember from being kids running in a field. Then there's talk of art and overwork, of children and the experience of aging. And sometimes things are said that make them want to stay and not go home.

If you'd like to enjoy the company of men, you don't need drums. You don't have to build a sweat lodge. All you need is a shared sport, like soccer, softball, tennis, rowing, volleyball, basketball, hockey, and so on. If you'd like to get a sports group or team going, we suggest you:

- Start by tapping your friends.

- Put an ad up at a local sporting goods store, gym, or park, or on a local community Internet site such as craigslist. Make sure the ad clearly states whether you want male players only, or are seeking a coed group. The dynamics will be quite different in each case. Whenever you meet someone you like, find out if that person plays the sport in question.

- Set a regular time to play or practice.

- Look for a spot you can hang out afterward, where you can cool down while all those endorphins cook up some lively conversation.

SPIRITUAL SUPPORT

More than twenty years ago, the Reverend Jim Glyer created something he called the Lenten Living Room Group. Essentially, it's a small prayer community that explores spiritual themes and provides support during the six-week Lenten season. This is the story of one of his living room groups.

In 1985, Jim Glyer and Dr. Patrick Horay started a group in Patrick's home. The five men who came that night expected it to last for just the forty days of Lent. Instead, it went on for fifteen years.

At the first meeting, each man described a problem or challenge that he was asking for the group's support to face. As he talked, each of the others wrote brief summaries of what was said in something called a "prayer request book." Each man promised that he would look daily at every name and request written in his book, holding it for a moment in his thoughts and prayers.

Over the years, Jim and Patrick's group took on a life and structure of its own. Each meeting began with a check-in regarding the previous week's prayer requests. What had changed? How did the person feel as he coped with the problem? What kind of grace or blessing had he found? Then they all sat down to dinner.

After dinner, each man shared his prayer requests for the next week. The rest of the group took notes in their books. There was no advice. Just an effort to understand. It was time then for the "closing circle." The group stood, holding hands. Between moments of silence, each of them offered brief, extemporaneous prayers. Some were only a few words—expressions of an awareness or a feeling. Some expressed simple longings. Some were murmurs of pain and loss or thoughts of loved ones. Some were shouts to heaven.

During their time apart, in addition to prayers for each other, group members read meditations in a publication called the *Daily Word*. Every day the meditation changed, but the men felt bonded by the knowledge that they were all reading the same thing at the same time.

Over the years, everyone in the prayer group has faced enormous challenges. Two have died of AIDS. One man struggles with Parkinson's disease. One required brain surgery. All have lost loved ones. But through it all they supported each other with prayer and by always being there when needed.

If you'd like to start your own prayer or spiritual support group, here are some beginning steps:

- Talk to friends who are spiritually oriented. Put the word out at your church.

- Make the group time-limited at first—perhaps six to ten weeks. Early meetings may go more smoothly if you use short readings or meditations as topics for discussion.

- Groups that have good chemistry will become ongoing (sometimes meeting less often). The need for "topics" will decline as more time is taken with prayer requests, check-ins, and group support.

- Use of the prayer request book is strongly recommended. Each member should have one, and use it daily to pray for other members.

- Groups that encourage a daily spiritual practice, such as the meditations used by Jim and Patrick's group, seem to offer more support for members. In the words of Patrick Horay, "a daily spiritual practice anchors and feeds your spirit—particularly when you share it with others."

- Here are some resources for daily prayers and meditations:

    1. *Day by Day*. 1998. Edited by Chaim Stern. Boston: Beacon Press.

    2. *The Color of Light*. 1988. Perry Tilleraas. New York: Harper Books.

    3. *Daily Word*. (Periodical published by Unity School, 1901 NW Blue Parkway, Unity Village, MO 64065.)

COMING OUT GROUP

"I remember how it was before I came out. I told my mom when I was seventeen and we were doing the dinner dishes. Just blurted it out. And without missing a beat my mom said, 'That's ridiculous, Alex. You can't even make up your mind about what college to go to, what major, what kind of ice cream you like. How in the world could you have decided you're gay?' I mumbled something like 'guess you're right,' just 'cause I wanted out of that conversation. After that we both acted like I'd never said it. But I knew I had. I picked a college and a major. And I started the GLBT group on my campus.

"I decided that no one I knew was going to feel isolated and alone or like a freak if I could help it. My first three months on campus, a guy on my dorm floor got harassed by two guys from a frat. I didn't know if he was gay or not. Didn't care, really. The point was that they thought he was and that made it okay to call him names and push him around. It made me so furious I could barely see. I had fantasies of pounding them into the pavement. Then I realized that the bigger goal would be to help everyone feel safe and accepted on the campus. I made an appointment to see the dean of student affairs and just laid it out for her, how everyone has rights—whether they are students, staff, or faculty—to be who they are and not be attacked for it, verbally or otherwise.

"I could see her giving me a good look (I wore eyeliner especially for this meeting) and I remember her listening really closely but not saying much. Finally she asked me what I wanted. And I told her: I wanted an office for a gay group on campus; and I wanted a budget to run the office, to sponsor dances and a banquet, and to put on educational and consciousness-raising programs. And I wanted there to be a zero tolerance policy toward harassment of gay, lesbian, bisexual, and transgendered people on campus.

"She smiled, very slightly, and said, 'So Alex, you want to start small.' I just grinned back. And that's how it all began."

⊙ If there isn't a GLBT group on your campus, find out who the appropriate person is to authorize one. Do campus groups need to be sponsored by a faculty person? If so, someone from the women's studies, psychology, sociology, or health education departments may be a good bet for support.

- Get clear about your goals and create a mission statement. Will the group's aim be political—to alter campus policy—or social—to give students a place to hang out—or a combination? Maybe there is a need for gay-oriented referrals and resources. The group can connect students with gay-friendly therapists and healthcare providers, provide books and pamphlets on safer sex, coming out, and GLBT activism, and publicize GLBT cultural events.

- Can students at your college get credit for doing volunteer work? If so, your GLBT group can help provide some of that work. For example, find out about setting up a "warm line" for students who are questioning their sexuality and who may be too shy to come to the office. The psychology department can help provide training for volunteers on how to handle calls and how to provide basic counseling and referrals.

- Have regular meetings with the staff and volunteers of the GLBT office, and plan regular events—whether setting up a coming out support group, doing a sensitivity training in a classroom, deciding how to participate in the local gay pride parade, or just having a Friday night pizza and beer get-together.

- Keep in touch with the dean who oversees campus groups. Good communication between you and the dean's office will help foster quick action in times of need.

- Do outreach by being visible to other gay-positive agencies and businesses such as local bookstores, health food stores, women's clinics, and gay and lesbian bars and coffeehouses. Make the brochures and contact information of these organizations available to students. Stay in touch with everyone. A community is many things, and your immediate group on campus should also extend to the wider community of your city.

THE DUMPED CLUB

Carl Jung once observed that "What has not been properly separated cannot be properly joined." He was talking about the importance of being truly independent—capable of nourishing and taking care of ourselves—as a prerequisite for healthy relationships. The Lebanese poet Kahlil Gibran said the same thing differently: "Love one another, but make not a bond of love. The oak tree and the cypress grow not in each other's shadow."

Rebecca hadn't read Jung or Gibran, but she had a pretty good idea why she was unhappy. In her past several relationships she'd clung to men who were emotionally distant and critical, even cruel. It seemed, looking back, that the less they gave, the more she hung on. Rebecca sensed intuitively that she needed to be strong and comfortable on her own before she could find a healthy partnership.

As a former civil rights organizer, Rebecca knew that any kind of change, even personal change, was more likely to happen with support. So she put an ad up at a women's health clinic, another at an artist's collective, and a third at a women's therapy center. The little sign read: "Tired of holding on to lousy relationships? Join a group of women supporting women to get stronger and more independent and to stop making the same mistakes. Free. Leaderless."

They met the first night at a big table in a coffee shop. Seven showed up. When Rebecca asked what each woman wanted from the group, there were answers like this:

"I'm sick of turning myself into a pretzel to please some shlub."

"I want my life, not his life."

"I want to take as good care of myself alone as I do of a guy."

"I'm done being a member of the Dumped Club."

"The Dumped Club" got a big laugh, and from then on it became the nickname for the group.

When the introductions were over, Rebecca asked each woman to talk about how she hoped the group could help her reach her goals. Here's what they said:

"You could help me see what I'm doing wrong. Then tell me when I'm about to do it again."

"Every man I meet, it's a different face but the same guy underneath. Help me stop that."

"My basic stance in the world is 'Excuse me for living.' When you're like that, even decent guys start treating you like crap. I need support to ask for what I want."

"When I'm alone, I just sit there watching TV. I need your support to start doing things for myself, to start having a life."

Though a few women came and went, the core group met for nearly three years. There was a lot of cajoling, confronting, suggesting—and laughing. "What I love most about this," one woman said, "is no one lets me get away with anything. They nail me the second I pull any of my old stuff."

"That's 'cause your old stuff is about as big and loud as a freight train. Can't miss it, sweetie. Not in the Dumped Club." There was a burst of laughter, and a few people in the coffee shop turned to look at the group. None of the women gave a damn.

If you want to start a women's group to support changing relationship patterns, you should:

- Advertise in women's health and therapy centers, women's bookstores, women's studies classes, and so on.

- Interview people on the phone. Listen to how they talk. Eliminate people whose speech seems pressured or who are very angry. They'll manipulate the group.

- In the first meeting, establish what everyone wants out of the group, and how they think the group can help them achieve their ends.

- Encourage every woman to form a personal plan for change that's built on specific things they've contracted with the group to do differently.

- Structure the group to periodically check in with each member about how she's implementing her plan for change.

- Make sure that the tone is constructive, never shaming or hurtful. While good groups often confront and suggest, they *always* support.

CHAVER MEANS "FRIEND"

Alan's father frequently asked, "Well, have you made any nice Jewish friends yet?" But it was difficult to make friends in a city, and although Alan was a member of a synagogue and attended services, after a year he still could not answer his father's concerned question with a confident "yes."

"I always felt that my spiritual life was nourished just by stepping into the synagogue. There's a hush and a murmur of everyone speaking in respectful voices—a sense that this really is a sacred space. I feel at peace the whole time I'm there. But when I leave, I feel I leave all that behind, too. I have friends of other faiths and I want to connect with other Jewish people, but I don't know how to get that connection except by being in the same physical space and knowing, well, that we all feel the same way. But I guess I would just like to know that for sure, that other people feel the way I do."

That was six months ago. In a burst of uncharacteristic sharing, Alan told an acquaintance, David, what he was feeling, the longing he had. David suggested that they both meet with the rabbi. That was how they learned about a chavurah. "It's from the Hebrew word *chaver* which means 'friend.' That's what you two are seeking, right?" The rabbi told them that no one had yet had the time to organize a chavurah, as the synagogue had been understaffed for quite some time. "If you have the time, you would be doing the congregation an enormous service. Unfortunately there are limits to what I can accomplish myself, but other synagogues have been able to do this; why not us?"

Alan and David used the books in the rabbi's study to read more on the concept of a chavurah. They learned that the practice of getting together in small groups to form friendships that were social, spiritual, and intellectual dated back to the early 1970s. Each discovered that there was room for their own personal interests: David liked to participate in potlucks and throwing parties for some of the Jewish holidays, while Alan was drawn to the stimulation of studying Jewish authors and Jewish spiritual traditions.

Alan mentioned the chavurah to James, a coworker at his office, and a lightbulb went on for James. He immediately drew up a long list of ways the members of his parish could stay connected with each other beyond attending weekly mass. A secretary for a nonprofit, James saw his church as a way to involve himself in social activism in a more hands-on way. The organizational skills he used at his job carried over into his work organizing a church group to serve meals to the homeless. In no time James was keeping track of who was picking up food that had been donated, who would do the cooking, and who would do delivery. All three, Alan, David, and James, impacted their respective religious communities in ways that brought the congregants together and made them feel closer and more connected.

- Religious community can be a kind of subcommunity within the main group of congregants. This can be particularly helpful to remember if your synagogue or church has a very large membership. It is easy for people to feel somewhat lost in a large group, even when they share something so important in common. Speak to the rabbi, minister, or priest of the congregation about your desire to combine the spiritual with the social in the larger congregation.

- Often, houses of worship send out flyers to members of the congregation on a regular basis. If so, find out who is in charge of this and work with them to encourage people to join you in the community-building work you've chosen.

- Decide on an idea that combines your religious or spiritual values with a means of social connection. Does your church need a place for single people to talk with each other? How about a place for interfaith families to meet each other and share concerns?

- Don't take on too much trying to organize a large congregation. Start small, with an idea for one group, and see what happens from there.

FAMILY CAMPING

It all began in the early seventies, when Virginia Satir noticed that many of her friends in the family therapy community were showing signs of burnout. Clearly, the helpers needed help themselves. So Virginia started taking backpacking trips into the mountains with these therapists and their families. Periodically through the day, and especially in the evenings around the campfire, she would work with them therapeutically.

After a few years she decided that she wanted to access more people. So instead of hiking and backpacking, Virginia and an expanded number of families pitched their tents and lived together in a campsite for a week, in what came to be known as Satir Family Camp (SFC).

Aside from the usual fun of camping out and sharing food together, this extended family met every morning to "check in." This was a time to share appreciations or irritations and concerns. It was also a time to make a request to do some "work," a family therapy session conducted by one of the facilitators (therapists chosen by Virginia), held in the open, with all campers welcome to attend.

Larry, Paula, and their two teenagers, Jason and Julia, had gotten a lot out of the time they spent at SFC. They had learned how to communicate well together as a family, and felt free discussing anything openly. So when Paula had to relocate from the West Coast for professional reasons, they decided to transplant the family camp tradition as well.

After getting settled in their new home, Paula started talking about the idea of a family camp with some new women friends in the company cafeteria. She got the same reaction as Larry had gotten when he broached the subject in the locker room of the local YMCA: puzzled looks. The combination of camping out and family therapy just didn't strike a familiar chord with their new acquaintances.

"I just don't get it," Paula was saying, sipping her coffee Sunday morning. "We know that family camp is a great idea."

"Yeah, Mom," Jason chimed in, "*we* know it, but it sounds kind of freaky to people around here."

"I think we need to go slow," Julia added.

"The kids are right," Larry said. "Let's start with something easy, like two families going for a picnic or a hike."

And that's what they did two weeks later. Larry had scouted out an easy half-hour hike to an idyllic spot near a lake. There were also picnic tables and barbecue pits available on site. In the afternoon, while the kids were frolicking around the lake and playing Frisbee, the adults gathered in the shade and chatted about this and that. Almost by chance, someone brought up a parenting issue—how to handle curfews—and that started the discussion.

In the winter, Paula organized several weekend ski trips to the mountains. They rented a large cabin near the ski slopes, and invited one or two families at a time to join them, sharing expenses. Evenings in front of the fireplace the adults would sip mulled wine and start to share stories. Inevitably, some family situations would be brought up, and a discussion ensued.

In the spring, Paula and Larry invited all the families they had spent time with to a big barbecue in the local park. Over potluck dessert, Paula made her announcement. There was a group campsite available for a week in August at a nearby state park, which could accommodate as many families as wanted to get together. The special feature of the gathering would be that everyone would gather at night around a communal campfire to share family stories. The teenagers cheered when it was announced that they could have their own independent campfire.

Several families were interested. And at the end of the camping week, at the last campfire, an ad hoc committee was formed to plan the following year's Family Camp. Additional ideas that came up included planning more structured activities for the kids, a gourmet feast for the last night of camp, and perhaps inviting a consultant to help with communication issues.

When starting to organize a family camping group:

- Begin by making time-limited commitments, such as hiking together for a day or renting a large cabin for the weekend.

- Allow plenty of unstructured time in camp, but require a commitment to come to the evening campfire.
- Once the core group is formed, new families should be invited by someone who is already part of the group.

NEIGHBORHOOD WATCH

Debra's eyes are red from crying, and her friend Sam holds on to her hand as she talks. "I don't know how you get over a thing like this. It makes me just want to up and move. Go somewhere like a small town where these things don't happen." This evening, Debra came home from working at the deli to find her front door lock broken and the television and stereo system gone. Her little house, an in-law apartment at the back of a large house, is a wreck. Her clothes have been rifled, her drawers upended onto the floor, spilling her underwear and socks into piles.

"The thing that gets me," Sam says, "is that, okay, the house is kinda hidden, but there are people around during the day, people who work late shifts, people with kids. Somebody *had* to have seen something. It makes me so angry."

"Maybe it isn't true," said Debra, "but I feel so alone. Like I was doing something wrong, like it wouldn't happen to anyone else. Why me? What did I do?"

The uniformed policewoman who is sitting at Debra's side taking notes for the report looks up at this. "First, you didn't do anything wrong. And second, there was a break-in the beginning of this month, about four blocks up the street here."

"I didn't know that," Debra says in a hushed voice. "I wish I had. I don't know what difference it would've made, but I wish I'd known."

"Could make a difference," Officer di Croce says. "If you want to do something, that is. The police can only do so much."

"I don't understand," Sam says. "You mean like we should get a gun?"

Office di Croce smiles. "Hold on. No, arming yourself or becoming some kind of vigilante is definitely not what I mean. I'm talking about putting together a neighborhood watch group. Neighbors learn how to help each other and then you help us, the police. We'll train you to become observant, to spot any kind of suspicious behavior or activity, and then how to inform the police. You know, in the U.S. there's about one cop for every 2,000 people. That gives you some idea as to why the police need your assistance and why these neighborhood watch groups work. I know this is real difficult right now, Debra, but after I finish this report I'll give you my card and if you feel like taking some action, you give me a call."

"You'll do it, right?" Sam asks Debra. He looks at the officer. "I'll do it. I'll definitely do it. Just tell me what's the next step." Debra gives a quavering smile and nods.

- Call your local law enforcement agency and tell them you would like to start a neighborhood watch group. They will put you in touch with the crime prevention unit, and you can work out the logistics of having an officer come to your meeting to speak about what a watch group is and what it does.

- Try to choose a date and time that you think will probably work for you and your neighbors. Choose where to hold the meeting. It can be in someone's home if the space is large enough, or at a local school or church.

- Inform your neighbors of the meeting. Put together a colorful flyer and go door-to-door, or post them in places where your neighbors are likely to see them: schools, churches, grocery stores, laundromats, restaurants, and so on. Try to reach as many people as you can. Don't forget the police station, as any neighbor who has just had a crime committed against him or her may be willing to join others to take action.

- Communicate with the police about any unusual, suspicious, or dangerous activities your watch group observes.

- For a successful watch group to be effective, neighbors need to know what is going on in their neighborhood. Everyone needs to stay alert and observant and share information with each other and the police.

- Encourage your neighborhood newspapers to report criminal activities and arrests in each edition.

ROLLERBLADE FUN GROUP

It wasn't so much her mother's illness and death that caused the depression. It was the isolation of her nonstop focus on her mother's care, first at home, then in the nursing facility. Some of Yana's friends had now drifted away; others remained, but the relationships seemed shallow, distant.

Three weeks after the funeral, Yana felt the strong need to get out—perhaps to go rollerblading like she used to in Golden Gate Park. Of her three friends, one had a back injury, one had to take her kid to soccer practice, and one was having an existential crisis that required large amounts of rest and marijuana. Yana went rollerblading alone.

The park was beautiful, the path dappled with sun and shadow. The air was cool, stinging her cheeks slightly as she pushed along. Joggers and other rollerbladers surged along the same path, sometimes passing within inches of each other. "Like fish in the sea," Yana thought. "Swimming in schools while still separate and alone."

It was during these melancholy ruminations that Yana noticed a little shop near the park. It was a hole in the wall that sold rollerblades and skateboards. Something made her go in. There were the usual display racks and cases, but near the front door she saw a bulletin board with notices for classes, vacant apartments, and an upcoming skateboard competition.

A strange impulse seized Yana, and she asked for a piece of paper from the clerk. On the back of a pink invoice form she wrote the following:

"Rollerblade club. Novice to intermediate. Meet 11:00 A.M. every Sunday at Bellingham and Ninth. Enjoy the park, feel safe, make friends."

The clerk stared at her. "That might work," he said. "Lots of people just getting into blades come in here. They don't know anybody—take classes so they don't have to skate alone."

He was right. The first week there were ten people on the corner of Bellingham and Ninth, mostly women, mostly novices. They skated all the way down to the old windmill, where they rested, sipped from water bottles, and talked. By the time they got back to Ninth Street, they felt the beginning of a real camaraderie.

That was three years ago. Today the group's still going, although it meets somewhere else. Twenty or thirty people show up every Sunday. While Yana doesn't go every week—she's married now—she returns often enough to keep up with her friends. And once a month she gives lessons.

"I have no idea what possessed me to put up that ad," Yana says. "I've never done anything like it before or since. At that exact moment I was thinking of my mom; thinking she'd be worried about me if she could see what kind of shape I was in. Maybe she helped me, because all of a sudden I asked for that piece of paper."

If you want to start a sports club of this kind, we suggest you try the following:

- Put an ad up in a gym or in stores that sell equipment for the sport.

- Set the meeting in a public place. If people might need more information, consider posting your e-mail address.

- Arrange either a destination or an after-event meeting place (such as a restaurant or bar) where people who want to can chat and hang out.

RUNNING GROUP

Andy was a cop in New Jersey for over thirty years before he retired to his dream house in Idaho. "The wife and I bought this little place so I could fish and do nothing out here. I had damn well earned it after dealing with the hard side of life for decades." A picture of Andy and his partner Mike in their younger days, both in uniform and grinning in front of the station house, adorns his fridge.

"Mike moved out here, too. He and his wife are just up that road. And you know what? It was great. For about four months. And then, man oh man, did the novelty ever wear off in a big way. I was driving my poor wife nuts, I was so bored. I was used to always having some kind of project. I mean jeez, how much fish can you catch and eat?

"So now . . . I run. That other picture on the fridge? That's me and Mike these days." The second picture shows two older men, same big grins, in shorts with race numbers plastered across their chests. "I got this running group, fifteen people—thirteen normals and two cops." Andy laughs. "Seriously. This is a great group of people. Our first marathon, we helped raise a bunch of money for the Arthritis Foundation and now our group is planning on running the AIDS Marathon in December in Hawaii.

"I'm in better shape now, in my sixties, than I was for most of my life. Now I've got goals, something to work toward, and interesting people to do it with. Lots of people who used to run all by their lonesome, and now we're a real group. And damn, we're going to Hawaii!"

Starting a running group—whether you decide to compete in races or not—has the benefit of keeping you in good health. You'll make a group of friends who keep each other motivated to keep going. Knowing that your group is waiting for you can help inspire you to leave the comfort of a warm bed on a chilly morning. Here are some tips to get you started:

- Visit a store in your city or town that specializes in running gear. The salespeople will be knowledgeable about running tips, trails, races, and equipment. A running store will also carry runners' magazines, calendars for local and state races, and flyers from people looking for training partners. If no one is advertising for someone to run with, put up a flyer of your own.

- People run for all sorts of reasons, but runners who want to join a running group are looking for something in particular. Competitiveness can be a good thing, but a running group should have a stated goal of helping each other stay motivated and interested in their own and each other's improvement. Being able to engage in lively conversations can really help those miles go by on the trails.

- Decide on a regular meeting spot that is close to the routes you will be running, like the parking lot of a local business, a coffee shop, or a mall. Remember that you will start your runs from here, so the routes shouldn't be difficult to get to.

- Get input from local runners about their favorite routes, so that you have a number to choose from. It is more fun (and more conducive to improvement) when the scenery, pace, and distances are varied. Route distances can be anywhere from two miles up to ten or more.

- The group should begin together, warming up for the first mile or so. Then smaller groups can take different routes or go at different paces. By mixing it up, runners can do short runs working up to a long run on the weekend, or they can work on improving their speed or stamina. This way, runners have a shared experience with the entire group as well as being able to set individual goals for the week, month, and year.

- Once everyone has cooled off after a run, head to a coffee shop to hang out and discuss how everyone's training went. This is a good time to share ideas about goals, the next race to shoot for, or even that marathon in Hawaii.

GRIEF SUPPORT GROUP

"Give sorrow words," Shakespeare said. "The grief that does not speak breaks the heart." That's what Maureen Sullivan believed when she let her friends know she was starting a widows and widowers group. They, in turn, passed the message on to more than a dozen folks who'd lost a spouse and needed both the companionship and the support of those who understood grief.

Many of the people Maureen recruited were already attempting to date and cope with the singles scene. But she was convinced that widows and widowers are fundamentally different from other single folk. Death has taken their partners; they have suffered neither the specific hurt nor the disillusionment of divorce. Many lack the hardened defenses of singles who are embittered by a cavalcade of broken loves. Widows and widowers struggle with grief, not with these other scars.

Maureen's group started meeting every Saturday night. The idea was to have a place to go on the one night a week when everyone loathes being alone. It was a potluck. Even kitchen phobic guys had to bring "food worth eating." After a few weeks at Maureen's, the group set up a plan for rotating the host duties.

Louise, a charter member, describes the early meetings as "a time of tears. Some of us were still raw, and it helped to just tell our story. Not all at once, but in bits and pieces over the weeks. We had a lot in common. Fred would tell a story that reminded me of something in my own experience, and, in turn, something I said would trigger a memory for Nancy. And so it went."

Over the months the focus shifted. There was less dredging of the past and more conversation, less catharsis and more laughter. What had been a support group to heal grief became a social club.

Maureen's widows and widowers group started in 1972. By 1976, everyone in the group had remarried—most to another member of the club. For the last thirty years, they've continued to meet, and the bonds formed in those early days of sadness have proved deep and unbreakable. Last year, the Christmas party was at Rockaway Beach in Pacifica, California. Louise's son keeps a picture of Louise and Ted, his stepdad, that was taken that night. They are smiling in that open, easy way people do when they're in the company of old friends.

If you'd like to start a grief support group, we suggest that you:

- Contact a local hospice organization or advertise through your church. Even word of mouth can work, as it did in Maureen's case.

- Meet for potlucks in someone's home. Sharing a meal can help with bonding. Rotate who hosts the meeting and the potluck.

- Ask each person to share the story of his or her loss. Encourage other members to chime in as they are reminded of something in their own experience. It's okay if people repeat things, because grief isn't a linear process. Sometimes a story has to be told over and over in different ways before someone can move through the mourning experience.

- Encourage tears. Crying with others is often far more cathartic than crying alone.

- Over time, as stories of the past come up less often, or are less intense, encourage laughter and chatting. Slowly let go of the focus on grief as friendships form and attention shifts to enjoyment of the here and now.

A MUSICIANS' GROUP

When the oxen were weak or the trail too steep, wagon train pioneers had to lighten the load. Typically, the last thing left behind was any musical instrument. That would be an act of extreme desperation, because playing music together was how people found peace at the end of the day. While a lot has changed in the twenty-first century, the joy of making music together is still shared by millions.

Ten years ago, Nancy gave up on city life. She moved to Graton, which boasts a two-block-long main street surrounded by orchards and horse pastures. It's the kind of place, she says, where it takes three hours to get out of the market because you're so busy talking to people. Where if you fell down on the street there'd be a stampede to help you up.

But every paradise has a flaw. Nancy loves music, and takes particular joy in playing the recorder. Unfortunately, most people in town couldn't tell a musical staff from something a shepherd uses. For the first year it wasn't a problem—Nancy was busy adjusting to her new life. There was the discovery, for example, that roosters actually do crow at five in the morning. As time went by, though, she longed for a group of friends to play with.

One day, for some reason, Nancy remembered a quote from Martin Luther that appeared in the hymnals she used as a child: "Music is the only art that can calm the agitations of the soul." It gave her an idea. Within five minutes she was on her computer, setting Luther's statement in large, bold type at the top of the page. Then she wrote: "Recorder group forming. Have fun with two-, three-, and four-part pieces. Blow your agitations away."

She put the sign up in the closest music store (over in Forestville) and in several local churches, and she had it distributed at a recorder class at Santa Rosa Community College. Then the calls began, and with them came a new problem: who to choose?

A recorder group is an intimate thing, Nancy says. You have to choose as much for personality as you do for musical ability, because each person in your group has the potential to be a good friend or a weekly pain in the backside. Nancy screened group members by playing duets with them once or twice, and then deciding who'd be invited to the regular practice night. She remembers one man who didn't make the cut. He apparently liked to eat sardines for snack food, and "his enthusiastic blowing made the den smell like a fishing trawler."

These days the recorder group has five regular members. In addition to the weekly practice, they play at weddings and fund-raisers, and recently were invited to do a performing tour of Italian cathedrals.

If you'd like to start a music group of your own, we suggest the following to get started:

- Have clear goals. Do you want a Saturday afternoon string quartet to play favorite pieces? Do you want your group to perform eventually? Do you want collaborators for songwriting?

- Advertise in music stores that sell either the instruments or the sheet music used in your group. You can also put the word out with music teachers you know, at music schools, or in music classes.

- Screen or audition people before promising anything. Make sure you 1) like each person, 2) share similar goals and tastes with the person, 3) have a sense of the person's capacity to work cooperatively, and 4) are comfortable with the person's level of ability.

- Set a regular practice time and place. If you use sheet music, one group member should be responsible for obtaining it.

- Support each other. Focus on the positive, and appreciate the progress each member makes on a piece.

- Have fun together: share some dessert after practice, perform for friends, have a picnic and play in the park, or record your best pieces.

SELECTED RESOURCES

BOOKS

Alinsky, S. D. 1971. *Rules for Radicals: A Pragmatic Primer for Realistic Radicals.* New York: Vintage Books.
    This is the classic text for anyone wanting to organize a community. Written by the man who organized the "Back of the Yards" community in Chicago, it contains a wealth of strategies and nuggets of hard-earned wisdom.
Kretzmann, J. P., and J. L. McKnight. 1993. *Building Communities from the Inside Out: A Path Toward Finding and Mobilizing a Community's Resources.* Chicago: ACTA Publications.
    The main thrust of this book involves *asset-based* community development—a strategy that seeks to build on what is already present in a community. The first step is using a *capacity inventory*, a tool that helps you to find out about the gifts and talents of local people.
Mattessich, P. W., and B. Monsey. 1997. *Community Building: What Makes It Work: A Review of Factors Influencing Successful Community Building.* Saint Paul, Minn.: Amherst H. Wilder Foundation.
    The most valuable part of this book is its examination of the factors related to a community's success. This involves looking at various characteristics of the community, the community building process, and the community organizers.

Stone, R., ed. 1996. *Core Issues in Comprehensive Community-Building Initiatives*. Chicago: Chapin Hall Center for Children.

This book is a compilation of essays focusing on theories of neighborhood change, neighborhood governance, economic context for community building, and community organizing.

Whitmer, C., ed. 1993. *In the Company of Others: Making Community in the Modern World*. New York: Putnam.

This book's thirty-two chapters cover a range of topics, from the need for community to the making of community to the dark side of community. The book has an appealing mix of theoretical and practical material. It also has a wealth of real-life examples, from Starhawk's coven to the dystopian Jonestown.

WEB SITES

www.commbuild.org

This Web site provides a wide range of resources and information about innovative community building efforts. The focus is on projects to revitalize poor neighborhoods and to improve the life circumstances of residents and their families.

www.aecf.org/initiatives/ntfd

This site describes the neighborhood transformation and family development initiative funded by the Annie E. Casey Foundation. The foundation is committing half of its grants toward helping neighborhoods become places where children and their families can flourish.

www.pewtrusts.com

The Pew Charitable Trusts' neighborhood preservation initiative (NPI) was set up in 1994 to help residents of diverse working-class neighborhoods strengthen the social, physical, and economic assets that make neighborhoods healthy and viable. Its goal is to determine the types of strategies that foster residents' engagement in neighborhood preservation.

www.communitybuilding.com

This site is an excellent source of information about building an online community. It offers articles and links to consultants and a directory of resources.

Peter D. Rogers, Ph.D., is the administrative director of Haight Ashbury Psychological Services. A longtime activist, community organizer, and retired psychotherapist, Dr. Rogers is the coauthor of the popular self-help books *When Anger Hurts*, *The Anger Control Workbook*, and *The Divorce Book*.

Lisa Frankfort, L.M.F.T., is a psychologist in private practice and clinic coordinator of Haight Ashbury Psychological Services. Lisa fosters a sense of community for the trainees and clientele of this important neighborhood service provider.

Matthew McKay, Ph.D., is the clinical director of Haight Ashbury Psychological Services, a longstanding low-fee, community-based clinic in San Francisco, California. The coauthor of more than twenty self-help books including *The Relaxation and Stress Reduction Workbook*, and *Self-Esteem*, Dr. McKay lives with his family in Berkeley, California.

Some Other New Harbinger Titles

The 50 Best Ways to Simplify Your Life, Item FWSL $11.95

When Anger Hurts Your Relationship, Item WARY $13.95

The Couple's Survival Workbook, Item CPSU $18.95

Loving Your Teenage Daughter, Item LYTD $14.95

The Hidden Feeling of Motherhood, Item HFM $14.95

Parenting Well When Your Depressed, Item PWWY $17.95

Thinking Pregnant, Item TKPG $13.95

Pregnancy Stories, Item PS $14.95

The Co-Parenting Survival Guide, Item CPSG $14.95

Family Guide to Emotional Wellness, Item FGEW $24.95

How to Survive and Thrive in an Empty Nest, Item NEST $13.95

Children of the Self-Absorbed, Item CSAB $14.95

The Adoption Reunion Survival Guide, Item ARSG $13.95

Undefended Love, Item UNLO $13.95

Why Can't I Be the Parent I Want to Be?, Item PRNT $12.95

Kid Cooperation, Item COOP $14.95

Breathing Room: Creating Space to Be a Couple, Item BR $14.95

Why Children Misbehave and What to do About it, Item BEHV $14.95

Couple Skills, Item SKIL $15.95

The Power of Two, Item PWR $15.95

The Queer Parent's Primer, Item QPPM $14.95

Call **toll free, 1-800-748-6273,** or log on to our online bookstore at **www.newharbinger.com** to order. Have your Visa or Mastercard number ready. Or send a check for the titles you want to New Harbinger Publications, Inc., 5674 Shattuck Ave., Oakland, CA 94609. Include $4.50 for the first book and 75¢ for each additional book, to cover shipping and handling. (California residents please include appropriate sales tax.) Allow two to five weeks for delivery.

Prices subject to change without notice.